BARTOLOMÉ DE LAS CASAS

AN INTERPRETATION OF HIS LIFE AND WRITINGS

N.V. VAN DE GARDE & CO'S DRUKKERIJ, ZALTBOMMEL

D. FR. BARTHOLOME DE LAS CASAS

Del Orden de Predicadores, Obispo de Chiapa
Varon apostolico, y el mas zeloso de la felicidad
de los Indios.
Nació en Sevilla el año de 1474, y murió en Mad
el de 1566.

BARTOLOMÉ DE LAS CASAS
AN INTERPRETATION OF HIS LIFE AND WRITINGS

BY

LEWIS HANKE
Director, Hispanic Foundation
The Library of Congress
Washington

With 4 plates

THE HAGUE
MARTINUS NIJHOFF
1951

Copyright 1951 by Martinus Nijhoff, The Hague, Netherlands
All rights reserved, including the right to translate or to
reproduce this book or parts thereof in any form

PRINTED IN THE NETHERLANDS

To the Memory
of
My Mother and Father

JOSEPH RUZICKA, INC.

PREFACE

The life of Bartolomé de Las Casas, one of the greatest and most controversial figures in the Spanish conquest of America, has never been written in definitive form. The usual information which a biographer would need in order to draw a full length portrait of him simply does not exist. No reliable painting of this Dominican friar has come down to us, no contemporary description of his physical appearance has yet been discovered, and little is known of the first quarter century of his life. Some of his most important treatises have never been published and a satisfactory edition of even his greatest work, the *Historia de las Indias,* is only just now being brought out in Mexico.

Yet enough has been printed on his desperate struggle to protect the Indians of the New World to make him almost as well-known as Cortez or Pizarro. His ideas, however, have not been carefully studied; indeed, Las Casas has found a place on the scene of world history largely because of his denunciation of the cruelties committed by his fellow-countrymen in America. This little volume is designed to focus attention on his principal contributions to political science, history, and anthropology, and the center of attention is the relationship between the American Indians and their conquerors at that decisive moment when the soldiers and missionaries of Spain were opening up a new continent peopled with natives of widely differing customs. These brief chapters should be considered no more than an introduction to the study of the contact of races in modern times, and the treatment given here will surely be revised and amplified by later students of this great theme in the history of the expansion of Europe.

The chapters presented here are based upon material delivered at the University of Virginia in the fall of 1948 as the James W. Richard Lectures, and I take this opportunity to acknowledge my debt of gratitude to that institution for encouraging me to set down these thoughts on the significance of Las Casas.

LEWIS HANKE.

TABLE OF CONTENTS

Chapter I

THE STRUGGLE FOR JUSTICE IN THE SPANISH CONQUEST OF AMERICA

Spaniards differ among themselves in many ways and on many subjects. So it has always been and so it is today, as the presence in the Americas of hundreds of Spain's best scientists, scholars, and creative artists who no longer care or dare to live in their homeland testifies. Most Spaniards, however, agree in one belief — that the discovery and colonization of the New World was their country's greatest and most significant contribution to the world. Of course they by no means agree on what precisely that contribution was and there have been some Spaniards, during and after the conquest, who bitterly and publicly protested part or all of Spanish policy and action in America. For Spaniards have never hidden from the world their robust and penetrating criticism of Spain. The phrase "My country, right or wrong!" could never have been struck off by a Spaniard. One of those popular sayings which reveals some of the basic wisdom of Spanish character puts it this way:

Si habla bien de Inglaterra, es inglés,
Si habla mal de Alemania, es francés,
Si habla mal de España, es español.
If one speaks well of England, he is an Englishman,
If one speaks ill of Germany, he is a Frenchman,
If he speaks ill of Spain, he is a Spaniard.

There is likewise among non-Spaniards a pretty general agreement that the American portion of her history was her most glorious period, although among these too there exists a wide divergence of opinion on the true nature of the Spanish conquest. The purpose of this book is to set before you my own conclusion on the controversial glory of Spain in America: my belief that the conquest was far more than a remarkable military and political exploit; that it was also one of the greatest attempts the world has seen to make Christian precepts prevail in the relations between peoples. This attempt showed itself basically as a spirited defense, by numbers of Spaniards, of the rights of the Indians, which rested on two of the most fundamental assumptions a Christian can make; namely, that all men are equal before God, and that a Christian has a responsibility for the welfare of his brothers no matter how alien or how lowly they may be. The greatest Indian defender of them all, Fray Bartolomé de Las Casas, stands at the heart of this struggle for justice.

In the written history of American the undeniable courage, spectacular daring and greed of the *conquistadores* have hitherto been emphasized, as well as the impressive stability of the far-flung empire which Spain brought within the orbit of European civilization and ruled for over three hundred years. But there is more than this to Spain's contribution to the New World. Other nations sent out bold explorers who established and plundered empires. But no other European people, before or since the conquest of America, threw itself into such a struggle for justice as developed among Spaniards shortly after the discovery of America and persisted throughout the sixteenth century. This first chapter attempts to examine that unique quality of Spanish effort and to show how it influenced Spanish action in America [1].

[1] A much more detailed account of the matters treated in this chapter has been given by the author in *La lucha por la justicia en la conquista de América* (Buenos Aires, 1949, Editorial Sudamericana). An English version, considerably reduced in size, has been issued by the University of Pennsylvania Press entitled *The Spanish Struggle for Justice in the Conquest of America* (Philadelphia, 1949).

The use of the word *justice* may seem peculiarly ironic in a discussion of so bloody and violent a conquest. Nevertheless the concept of justice, as understood by the Spanish nation, which lived and thought within its framework of sixteenth-century Catholicism, must be regarded as an essential concept underlying the whole Spanish approach to the New World.

The concern that all Spain's laws and actions in America should be just was certainly not felt by all Spaniards. An extraordinary variety of men was drawn to the strange shores of the New World when the news of the discovery spread like wildfire across Europe. Some were the very scum of Spain, foot-loose ex-soldiers, broken noblemen, adventurers, or even convicts with clipped ears. Others were from the hardy peasant class who were on the make and who saw in America a chance to break their semi-feudal bonds. Fernando Cortés, who came from a relatively humble class, and Francisco Pizarro, who was a pig-herder in Spain, were the first "self-made Americans" of note.

Friars and priests also hastened to the lands across the sea for they hoped to win millions of new souls for the faith, and were given an opportunity to push out the frontiers of Christendom such as had rarely before been offered. And to operate the complicated machinery required to administer the vast territory now subject to the Spanish crown, royal officials were appointed who were to keep the balance among all these contending and contradictory groups.

The government of the New World was by no means a simple matter, because the bull of Alexander VI in 1493 and later papal grants conferred upon Spain a unique species of dominion, both ecclesiastical and political. Thus the crown, in fulfilling its responsibility to Christianize the Indians, found itself confronted by all manner of ecclesiastical disputes, as well as by difficult political problems.

How much religious instruction should Indians receive before baptism, should newly-won converts be required to pay tithes, and should the Inquisition be established in America to protect the Indians from heresy?

All these and many other ecclesiastical matters were considered by the Spanish authorities, from the king downward through the Council of the Indies, the principal governing body resident in Spain, the viceroys sent to the New World to represent the king, and the whole complicated hierarchy of lesser officials who checked and double-checked each other's activities. As the eighteenth-century Scottish historian William Robertson wrote: "The Spanish monarchs, having acquired a species of dominion formerly unknown, formed a plan for exercising it to which nothing similar occurs in the history of human affairs" [1].

All persons who wanted to achieve justice in America naturally turned to the crown in Spain as having both the power and responsibility to determine the course of events. What constituted justice and how it could be achieved were questions raised with every important step Spaniards took in the discovery, colonization and administration of their new dominions. This preoccupation with justice, which can only be understood in relation to the political and spiritual climate of opinion in sixteenth-century Spain, to be described presently, led to sharp and basic controversies on a variety of particular issues.

What political and economic rights should Spain enjoy from her overlordship there? Were the Indians rational beings, and, if so, what were their rights? How should the faith be preached to them; under what circumstances could they be made to work for Spaniards, and when could war be justly waged against them? All these and other questions were asked and heatedly

---

[1] Robertson, *History of America,* II (London, 1777), 353.

debated throughout the sixteenth century in both Spain and America and by all classes and manner of men.

The struggle for justice continued during the second half of the sixteenth century, and spread from the islands of the Caribbean to Mexico, Peru, and even to the distant Philippines. Wherever Spaniards carried their banners in the New World opened up by their energy and daring, there also they carried the ideas and concern for justice which led inevitably to those bitter controversies which endow the Spanish experience in America with original characteristics.

Learned controversies have long raged, and their fires are not yet quenched, over many of the men and events to be discussed in these chapters. Besides the usual doubts and disagreements that spring up among historians, no matter what the subject, those who write the history of Spain in America have often been subject to the special hazard of strong religious or political bias. On this account the struggle for justice has been one of the topics in Spanish history most vulnerable to partisan treatment.

Historians, especially those writing in English, even when they have recognized the existence of Spanish theories dealing with Spain's American problems, have usually confined themselves to pointing the finger of scorn, to show how far Spanish practice in America departed from the theory elaborated by the crown in Spain. The Spaniards' concern to work out a policy which they could justify to their own consciences has been dismissed as hypocritical religiosity akin to the spirit of the walrus in „Alice in Wonderland", who shed such bitter tears while busily assisting the carpenter to consume so many oysters. Thorstein Veblen faithfully represented a large body of opinion — outside Spain at least — when he asserted: „The Spanish enterprise in colonization was an enterprise in pillage, inflamed and inflated by religious fanaticism and martial vanity" [1].

Spanish ,,revisionists", eager to justify their ancestors' ways and to combat the "black legend" of Spanish cruelty and oppression in America, have replied to these critics by quoting long extracts from the humanitarian laws of the Indies with intent to prove the just and enlightened nature of the Spanish conquest and colonial system. Or they point out that other European nations were at least as cruel as the Spaniards, a characteristic defense by accusation which appeared most recently in the volume entitled *The Rise of the Spanish American Empire* [2] by the brilliant Spanish controversialist Salvador de Madariaga.

My ideal has been to follow the counsel of Fernando de los Ríos, the eminent Spanish scholar who first helped me years ago in Spain and who recently died in New York, whose writings led me to enquire into this subject. He urged: "Let us judge the Spanish colonial activities, not as Catholics or Protestants, but as observers with the objectivity necessary to those who propose to study a problem of great significance in history [3]".

The almost incredible story of the amusing, curious, and tragic episodes which took place when theories decided upon in Spain were put into practice in America cannot be understood except in relation to the climate of opinion prevailing in sixteenth-century Spain.

It was an age of theologians who believed that their duties and functions extended over a field so vast that no argument and no discussion was alien to the practice and purpose of theology. Their importance was so widely recognized in that century that even frontier officials in Florida felt the need of a theologian in their midst and requested the crown to send them one.

---

[1] Wesley Mitchell (ed.), *What Veblen Taught* (New York, 1936) 370.

[2] London 1947.

[3] "The religious character of colonial law in sixteenth-century Spain", *Proceedings of the sixth international congress of philosophy*, 1926 (1927), 483.

Religiosity was an integral and vital part of Spanish life. Captains of slaving ships promulgated and enforced strict laws against blasphemy and card playing. Even while Sir Francis Drake was raiding the Spanish coast, Philip II took time to consider how the sailors on the Armada could be kept from swearing. Another example of the strength of religious formalism has been well described by Alonso de Ercilla in his great epic poem *La Araucana* (1569) on the conquest of Chile [1]. The Araucanian chief Caupolicán had been captured and was about to be put to death when he expressed a desire to be baptized and become a Christian. "This caused pity and great comment among the Castilians who stood around," according to Ercilla, and Caupolicán was baptized "with great solemnity, and instructed in the true Faith as well as possible in the short time available." After this, the Spaniards made him sit on a sharp stake and shot him to death with arrows.

Sixteenth-century Spaniards were thoroughly saturated also with the spirit of legal formalism, and the New World offered many opportunities for the exercise of juridical formalities. Spaniards were so accustomed to certifying every action they took that notaries were as indispensable to their expeditions as friars and gunpowder. The *Requirement* or proclamation to be read to the Indians before warring against them was probably the best example. So familiar did the Indians become with this habit that they fled at once upon observing Spaniards draw out a piece of paper, for bitter experience had taught them that such ceremonies usually portended an assault against them [2]. Thus did the ritual of red tape come to America!

The extraordinary concern for legality of even the Spanish soldier is illustrated by the account Bernal Díaz

---

[1] Canto 34.

[2] Las Casas, *Apologética historia* (Madrid, 1909), 644–646.

has given of the encounter between his captain Fernando Cortés and the Indians at Cholula. Cortés explained to the Indians that "he had been sent to these countries to give them warning and to command them not to worship idols, nor sacrifice human beings or eat their flesh, or practice sodomy or other uncleanness" and urged the Indians to render obedience to the king of Spain. The Indians refused to give up their idols but "as to rendering obedience to our king, they were content to do so. And thus they pledged their word, but it was not done before a notary"[1].

But it was not done before a notary! Would a pikeman of any other European nation have noticed, let alone recorded, such a fact? And one cut-throat conquistador in South America, Lope de Aguirre, even took the trouble to rebel against his king in a legal way, drawing up, while deep in the Amazonian jungle, a manifesto which announced to the crown that he no longer considered himself subject to Spanish law.

The element of Spanish character which most deeply affected the struggle for justice in America is what Spanish and foreign interpreters alike have termed its "tendency toward polarization, a native passion for extremes". All the great figures of the conquest were moved by one or the other of two dominant and diametrically opposed motives.

The conquistador Francisco Pizarro once replied to an ecclesiastic in his company who was protesting the despoilment of Indians in Peru and urging upon him that God and the faith ought rather to be made known to them: "I have not come for any such reasons. I have come to take away from them their gold"[2].

---

[1] Bernal Díaz del Castillo, *Historia verdadera de la conquista de la Nueva España*, I (México, 1943), 228–229. Edited by Ramón Iglesia.

[2] This statement appears in an undated memorial sent to the king by Bernardino de Minaya, Archivo General de Simancas, Sección de estado, legajo 892, fol. 197 ff.

There it is in its stark simplicity, the oldest and most familiar motive for conquest. But it is deeply significant that the incident showing this motive cannot even be recounted without involving the second one, best set forth in a statement made by the Friar Bartolomé de Las Casas, who cried:

> The aim which Christ and the Pope seek and ought to seek in the Indies — and which the Christian Kings of Castile should likewise strive for — is that the natives of those regions shall hear the faith preached in order that they may be saved .... And the means to effect this end are not to rob, to scandalize, to capture or destroy them, or to lay waste to their lands, for this would cause the infidels to abominate our faith [1].

Here the other face of sixteenth-century Spanish character looks boldly at us, and the second motive compelling Spaniards during the conquest reveals itself: the missionary urge to carry to far places and hitherto unknown men the great message from Christendom — the faith.

Between the two poles — the thirst for gold and the winning of souls, not for Spain, I should like to stress, but for the glory of God — a variety of mixed motives appeared. Some conquistadores were at times as missionary-minded as the most devoted friars. A few ecclesiastics were as worldly as Pizarro in their search for wealth and a life of ease in America. Many Spaniards, however, exemplified both motives. As the classic statement by Bernal Díaz put it: "We came here to serve God and the king, and also to get rich" [2].

The historian today would know much less about the struggle for justice if the Spaniards had not discussed

---

[1] Las Casas, *Colección de tratados* (Buenos Aires, 1924), 561, 617.
[2] Bernal Díaz del Castillo, *op. cit.*, II, 394.

their American problems so freely and so frankly. Throughout the sixteenth century, ecclesiastics, conquistadores, colonists, Indians, and a multitude of royal officials from all the far corners of Spain's New World empire sent messages to the king and the Council of the Indies, explaining what and who was wrong and describing the measures required to remedy the situation. What makes the relative freedom of speech enjoyed in sixteenth-century America so notable is that the Spanish rulers not only permitted but encouraged it. The historian who digs away today in the great Archive of the Indies in Seville becomes painfully aware of the results of this policy, for literally tons of reports and letters of the most controversial and divergent nature have been preserved there on every aspect of colonial administration.

The period in which Spaniards expressed their views most freely coincided with the greatest age Spain has ever known, and some Spaniards well understood that this was no accidental relationship. The plain speaking of sixteenth-century Spaniards must be considered — along with the legal formalism, religiosity, devotion to theology, and passion for extremes — as an important element in the climate of opinion which prevailed during the momentous epoch which Spaniards considered the Eighth Wonder of the World — the discovery and conquest of America.

Spaniards not only spoke freely on American problems, they also wrote extensively and heatedly on American history as they were making it. One great topic touched upon by every historian or free-speaking Spaniard was the true nature of the Indians. No other controversy so universally embroiled Spaniards during the sixteenth century or so well illustrates the climate of opinion.

From the very beginning of the conquest, opinion was sharply divided concerning the nature of the Indians — particularly their capacity to live according to the ways of the Spaniards and their ability to receive the Christian faith. As the discovery and colonization proceeded, the treatment of the Indians became an issue of prime importance, for the proper treatment to be accorded the Indians, the proper laws to be devised to govern them, depended to a large degree on their nature, or at least upon the Spaniard's concept of their nature.

Though more subtle, more moderate, and more realistic theories were eventually developed, the majority of the Spaniards in the Indies during the first half century of the conquest tended to look upon the natives either as "noble Indians" or as "dirty dogs".

Bartolomé de Las Casas may be taken as an extreme example of the "noble Indian" group when he cried:

> God created these simple people without evil and without guile. They are most obedient and faithful to their natural lords and to the Christians whom they serve. They are most submissive, patient, peaceful and virtuous. Nor are they quarrelsome, rancorous, querulous or vengeful. Moreover, they are more delicate than princes and die easily from work or illness. They neither possess nor desire to possess worldly wealth. Surely these people would be the most blessed in the world if only they worshipped the true god [1].

Gonzalo Hernández de Oviedo y Valdés, official historian and sworn foe of Las Casas, was one of the most prominent among the rival school. He considered the Indians "naturally lazy and vicious, melancholic, cowardly, and in general a lying, shiftless people. Their marriages are not a sacrament but a sacrilege. They are idolatrous, libidinous, and commit sodomy. Their chief desire is to eat, drink, worship heathen idols, and commit bestial

---

[1] Las Casas, *Colección de tratados,* pp. 7–8.

obsenities"[1]. What could one expect from a people whose skulls are so thick and hard that the Spaniards had to take care in fighting not to strike on the head lest their swords be blunted?

Here we have a classic statement of the two extreme points of view which agitated many Spaniards from their earliest contacts with the Indians. Practically every important figure in the New World and many in Spain delivered a judgment on the capacity of the Indians. Humble friars and renowned theologians, such as Francisco de Vitoria at the ancient University of Salamanca, arose to defend the Indians from the charge of irrationality. One of the greatest battles on the nature of the Indians, which will be described later in the third chapter, took place in Valladolid in 1550 and 1551 when Juan Ginés de Sepúlveda and Las Casas fought bitterly over the question whether the Aristotelian theory that some men are by nature slaves was applicable to the Indians.

As indicative of the bitter and open conflict that raged on the subject, a conflict which still divides historians and influences their history, the deathbed retraction by Friar Domingo de Betanzos of his previous opinion that the Indians were beasts may be cited. Betanzos had been instrumental in persuading Las Casas to become a friar, had later reproved Las Casas for his "indiscreet zeal," had labored in the Indies for thirty-five years, and now in 1549 returned to Spain on his way to die in the Holy Land. After going on foot from Seville to Valladolid he stopped at the San Pablo monastery where death overtook him. But before this occurred, a solemn and impressive drama was enacted.

Surrounded by his Dominican brothers, Betanzos repudiated the idea that the Indians were beasts. In the

---

[1] This estimate has been compiled from Oviedo's remarks in his *Historia general y natural de las Indias* (Madrid, 1851), Primera parte, Lib. 2, cap. 6; Lib. 4, cap. 2; Lib. 5, Prohemio, caps. 2–3; Lib. 6, cap. 9.

words of the notary who was called to witness this event and whose formal record of it was discovered not long ago in a Bolivian monastery:

> In the very noble city of Valladolid on September 13, in the year of Our Lord 1549, before me Antonio Canseco, notary public of Your Majesties, being in the monastery of San Pablo of the Order of Preachers, in a room in that monastery there was an old man with head and beard shaven, lying in bed apparently ill but in his right mind, called Friar Domingo de Betanzos. And he handed over to me, the aforesaid notary public, a sheet of paper on which he told me he had written and declared certain matters which concerned his conscience, and which related especially to the affairs of the Indies, which manuscript and declaration he delivered to me [1].

This declaration referred to a written memorial Betanzos had presented to the Council of the Indies some years before in which he had declared that the Indians were beasts (*bestias*), that they had sinned, that God had condemned them, and that all of them would perish. Now on his deathbed he believed that he had erred "through not knowing their language or because of some other ignorance" and formally retracted the statements in the memorial.

A few days after signing this declaration, Betanzos died. For him the struggle was resolved. His Dominican brothers, who doubtless were largely responsible for the whole episode, hastened to make sure that his final statement was made public and that the Council of the Indies received a duly certified copy.

But the issue was not resolved for the king, the Council of the Indies, and all those concerned with the administration of the New World. One of the ablest administrators Spain sent to America, Antonio de Mendoza,

[1] This manuscript is in the Convento de San Felipe in Sucre, Bolivia.

the first Viceroy of New Spain, arrived at what seems to us today a common sense conclusion on the question. Writing a formal memorial of advice to his successor, about the time that the friar Betanzos made his retraction in Valladolid, Mendoza recommended that neither those Spaniards who considered the Indians simple, industrious, humble, without malice or evil, or those who held the contrary view should be believed. "Treat the Indians like any other people," he urged, "and do not make special rules and regulations for them. There are few persons in these parts who are not motivated, in their opinion of the Indians, by some interest, whether temporal or spiritual, or by some passion or ambition, good or bad" [1].

Some Spaniards in America followed this wise counsel of moderation, but most did not and all continued to grapple with the problem which was directly or indirectly related to practically every event in the history of the struggle for justice, to which we now turn.

The Spanish conscience had been twinged by American events early in the conquest, for searching questions had been raised concerning the first Indians to reach Spain. Columbus paraded these natives through the streets of Seville and Barcelona on his first triumphal return, to whet the popular interest in his enterprise and to win royal support for further adventuring in the New World. He also sent back to Spain, after his second voyage, a consignment of natives to be sold as slaves, a clear hint concerning the financial possibilities of the land. The crown ordered Bishop Juan Rodríguez de Fonseca on April 12, 1495, to sell these Indians, but on the following day another dispatch instructed him to hold the money received from the sale until theologians could satisfy the royal conscience concerning the morality of the act.

---

[1] *Documentos inéditos de América,* VI, 499.

The first two decades of Spanish rule was a period of almost unchecked exploitation of the Indians. The needy adventurers who rushed to America were in no mood to treat the Indians tenderly or consider their rights. One eye-witness of those turbulent days reported that one could see riffraff who had been scourged or clipped of their ears in Castile lording it over the native chiefs in the New World. Many of the Spaniards had taken Indian women to serve them as concubines and this fact naturally helped to embitter relations between Spaniards and native men. Food also ran short, one crisis after another developed, and Indian labor was increasingly drafted to hunt for gold or to grow crops for Spaniards.

The *encomienda* system then was evolved, as the practical result of the responsibility of the crown to Christianize the Indians and the need of the Spaniards for someone to labor on their behalf. The theory of the encomienda was simple. The Spanish crown gave or "commended" Indians to Spaniards, who became *encomenderos,* and this grant gave the Spaniards the right to exact labor or tribute from the Indians. In return, the encomenderos were obligated to provide religious instruction for their Indians and to protect them. The encomenderos also, as the system developed, came to owe an obligation to the king, that of defending the land.

In practice, the encomienda system was established by Columbus in 1499 after the failure of his attempt to impose a definite tribute on the Indians of Hispaniola. The pattern evolved that in the islands, where there were relatively few Indians, many of whom died promptly under Spanish rule, service rather than tribute was rendered, whereas on the mainland the encomenderos enjoyed both tribute and service from the Indians and were thus enabled to lead a relatively dignified and comfortable life under semifeudal conditions. The encomienda, then, started with Columbus, when he assigned three hundred Indians to Spaniards. When Queen Isabella learned this, she asked her famous question: ..By what authority does the Admiral give my vassals away?"

The encomienda was put on an institutional basis by the first royal governor, Nicolás de Ovando, who arrived in April 1502 at Hispaniola, principal seat of Spanish government during the first quarter century after 1492. A great company of men was with him, some twenty-five hundred in all, probably including Las Casas, but none of them had come to labor with their hands. Ovando carried instructions to take away the Indians from Spaniards, put them under the crown, and require them to pay tribute out of the daily wages they would earn. This attempt failed, and by royal order of December 20, 1503, Ovando was permitted to grant Indians.

> Because of the excessive liberty the Indians have been permitted, they flee from Christians and do not work. Therefore they are to be compelled to work, so that the kingdom and the Spaniards may be enriched, and the Indians Christianized. They are to be paid a daily wage, and treated as free persons for such they are, and not as slaves [1].

So runs the royal order.

The theory of the encomienda may have been splendid, but in practice it did not serve in those early years to protect the Indians, and with the coming of the Dominicans to Hispaniola the protests against the Spanish treatment of the natives began to mount.

On the Sunday before Christmas in 1511, a Dominican friar named Antonio de Montesinos preached a revolutionary sermon in a straw-thatched church on the island of Hispaniola. Speaking on the text "I am a voice crying in the wilderness," Montesinos delivered the first impor-

---

[1] *Ibid.*, XXXI, 209–212.

tant and deliberate public protest against the kind of treatment being accorded the Indians by his Spanish countrymen. This first cry on behalf of human liberty in the New World was a turning point in the history of America and, as the late Pedro Henríquez-Ureña termed it, one of the great events in the spiritual history of mankind [1].

The sermon, preached before the "best people" of the first Spanish town established in the New World, was designed to shock and terrify its hearers. Montesinos thundered, according to Las Casas:

> In order to make your sins against the Indians known to you I have come up on this pulpit, I who am a voice of Christ crying in the wilderness of this island, and therefore it behooves you to listen, not with careless attention, but with all your heart and senses, so that you may hear it; for this is going to be the strangest voice that ever you heard, the harshest and hardest and most awful and most dangerous that ever you expected to hear .... This voice says that you are in mortal sin, that you live and die in it, for the cruelty and tyranny you use in dealing with these innocent people. Tell me, by what right or justice do you keep these Indians in such a cruel and horrible servitude? On what authority have you waged a detestable war against these people, who dwelt quietly and peacefully on their own land? .... Why do you keep them so oppressed and weary, not giving them enough to eat nor taking care of them in their illnesses? For with the excessive work you demand of them they fall ill and die, or rather you kill them with your desire to extract and acquire gold every day. And what care do you take that they should be instructed in religion? .... Are these not men? Have they not rational souls? Are you not bound to love them as you love yourselves? Be certain that, in such a state as this, you can no more be saved than the Moors or Turks [2].

---

[1] *Literary currents in Hispanic America* (Cambridge, 1945), 15.

[2] *Ibid.*, 15–16. The report of the sermon is given by Las Casas in *Historia de las Indias*, Lib. 3, cap. 4. Other information on this episode is given in Lib. 3, caps. 3–12, 17–19, 33–35, 81–87, 94–95.

Montesinos thereupon strode out of the church with head high, leaving a muttering crowd of colonists and officials behind him, who were astounded, but not one was converted. He had come as near to convincing his hearers of their wrong-doing as would a theological student in our day who delivered a soapbox philippic in Wall Street on the Biblical text "Sell whatsoever thou hast and give to the poor, and thou shalt have treasure in heaven."

The colonists gathered at the house of the governor, Diego Columbus, protested against the sermon as a scandalous denial of the lordship of the king in the Indies, and delegated a group which went indignantly to the monastery to exact an apology and disavowal. The vicar, Pedro de Córdoba, unimpressed by the delegation's threat to expel the offensive friar, assured them that Montesinos had spoken for the Dominican group. He promised, however, that Montesinos would preach the next Sunday on the same topic. The colonists thereupon retired, believing they had won their point.

Word of the expected retreat spread quickly, and the following Sunday most of the leading Spaniards crowded into the church. Montesinos mounted the pulpit and announced the disquieting text, "Suffer me a little and I will show thee that I have yet to speak on God's behalf." Rather than explaining away his previous sermon with dialectic subtleties, he proceeded to belabor the colonists anew, with even more passion than before, warning them that the friars would no more receive them for confession and absolution than if they were so many highway robbers. And they might write home what they pleased, to whom they pleased.

These words were soon heard in Spain, even by the king. On March 20, 1512, Ferdinand ordered the Admiral Diego Columbus to reason with Montesinos. If the Dominican and his brothers persisted in their error, previously condemned by the canonists, theologians and learned men gathered to deliberate on the problem ten years before, the Admiral was instructed to ship them to Spain by the first ship so that their superior might punish them "because every hour that they remain in the islands holding such wrong ideas they will do much harm" [1].

Three days later on March 23, 1512, the Dominican superior in Spain, Alonso de Loaysa, reproved Montesinos in an official communication to the Dominican provincial in Hispaniola and ordered him to prevail upon his friars to stop preaching such scandalous doctrine. The provincial was warned that no more friars would be sent if such preaching were permitted to continue. Thus began the first great struggle for justice in the New World.

Perhaps the general indifference during those early years to the sufferings of the Indians and unconcern with their rights are best illustrated by the attitude of Bartolomé de Las Casas, later one of the most remarkable and controversial figures of the conquest. From his boyhood in Seville he had had some familiarity with American problems and with Indians. He was present in Seville when Columbus, on his return from his first voyage in 1493, triumphantly exhibited through the streets natives and parrots from the New World. His father accompanied Columbus on the second voyage and is supposed to have given him an Indian slave to serve as page during his student days at the University of Salamanca. Las Casas himself went to America, probably with Ovando in 1502, and was not much better than the rest of the gentlemen-adventurers who rushed to the New World, bent on speedily acquiring fortunes. He obtained Indian slaves, worked them in mines, and attended to the cultivation of his estates. The affairs of the young university graduate prospered. While he did not mistreat his

---

[1] José María Chacón y Calvo, *Cedulario cubano* (Madrid, 1930), 431.

Indians, no doubts concerning the justice of his actions disturbed him even through he had become a priest. In 1512 he participated in the conquest of Cuba and received as a reward both land and the service of some Indians.

It was against such men as the Las Casas of those early days of the conquest that Montesinos raised his voice. And Las Casas shared the resistance of the other colonists to the message of Montesinos, for he, like them, took no steps to change his way of life and for more than two years after the sermons continued to play the role of comfortable gentleman-ecclesiastic, although once during this time he was refused the sacraments by a Dominican because he held slaves. The hot dispute that ensued left him disturbed but unconvinced.

But the seed of a great decision must have been growing within this obstinate man, as yet unaware that his destiny was to become the greatest Indian champion of them all. It was while he was on his estate in Cuba near the Arimao River preparing a sermon he was to deliver on Whitsunday of 1514 at the newly established settlement of Sancti Espiritus that his eye fell upon this verse in Ecclesiasticus: "He that sacrificeth of a thing wrongfully gotten, his offering is ridiculous, and the gifts of unjust men are not accepted".

Pondering on this text for several days and turning over in his mind the doctrines preached by the Dominicans, Las Casas became increasingly convinced "that everything done to the Indians thus far was unjust and tyrannical". The scales fell from his eyes, he saw at last what was to be forever after the truth for him, and experienced as complete a change of life as did Saul of Tarsus on the road to Damascus.

Characteristically he did not shrink from entering upon the new life immediately. He gave up his Indians, and preached a sermon at Sancti Espiritus against his fellow Spaniards which shocked them as much as the words of Montesinos had surprised and alarmed his congregation. Henceforth Las Casas devoted his life to the Indians, and in every book he read "whether in Latin or in Spanish, he found additional reasons and authorities to prove and corroborate the justice of those Indian people and to condemn the robbery, evil, and injustice committed against them" [1].

He was to follow this path, chosen in his fortieth year, for the remaining more than fifty years of his life, and the energy and skill hitherto employed for his own comfort and enrichment were to lead him to far places and very many times across the Ocean Sea to attack and astonish generations of his countrymen. It is not too much to say that the struggle for justice which this book recounts would have been much less stoutly and less persisten ly fought without him, that indeed, the story of the struggle becomes to a considerable extent the story of his life.

And yet the struggle was larger than any one man. It is symbolic that it was touched off by an almost unknown friar. No writings of Montesinos have come down to us, nor any picture of him, and of his life after the famous sermons we know little, except that he spoke at the court in Spain on behalf of the Indians and met his death while protecting them in Venezuela. Millions of Americans today have never heard his name. Our only records of his great moment in history appear in the royal instructions ordering him to be silent and in the *History of the Indies* by Las Casas whose description, written four hundred years ago, conveys to us vividly the passion and the force of this first blow struck for human freedom in America.

The struggle for justice can best be understood, how-

---

[1] The story of Las Casas' early life is based on his *Historia de las Indias*, Lib. 3, caps. 28–32, 79–80.

ever, through the work of Las Casas, for he wrote more copiously, spoke more vigorously, and lived longer than any other prominent figure of the conquest. He was no scholar of the closet but a tenacious, dynamic fighter who was always eager to put into practice the doctrines he preached. His life can best be summed up by describing the ways by which he attempted to save the Indians, in a series of audacious experiments for which he was able to obtain official support.

The first proposal by Las Casas which won royal approval failed completely when put to the test. His plan, which was the culmination of several years of agitation at court, was to colonize in 1521 the northern coast of Venezuela, then called Tierra Firme, with Spanish farmers who would till the soil, treat the Indians kindly, and thus lay the basis for an ideal Christian community in the New World. The colony was such a complete and humiliating failure that Las Casas retired to a monastery, entered the Dominican Order, and for almost ten years kept himself apart from affairs of this world.

The vision which guided Las Casas was of a New World in which Spanish farmers, transplanted with tools, seeds and supplies furnished by their king, their native industry, farming ability and firmness in the faith being their own contribution, would take root in America. They would till the soil of Tierra Firme and live side by side with the Indians there in such a way that their faith and their skill and industry would insensibly be absorbed by the natives and an ideal Christian community would come into being. The poor and lowly peasants of Spain would enjoy an opportunity to improve themselves in America, these industrious people would develop the king's newly discovered lands, thus increasing royal revenue, and above all the natives would be Christianized, not brutalized or despoiled of their wives and property.

The practice of bringing sturdy folk who would do

their own work, if extended throughout Spain's empire, would make unnecessary the encomienda system by which Indians labored for Spaniards. The experiment was as bold in its own way as two other great deeds which occurred at about the same time — the circumnavigation of the world by Magellan's men, and the victory over Montezuma and his hosts by Cortés.

The colonization plan failed, partly because the conditions stipulated by Las Casas as necessary to launch the project did not exist. Spaniards willing to risk their lives and fortunes in the New World were interested, not in becoming farmers, even if they had been such in Spain, but in becoming men of wealth and position. Cortés well expressed this feeling when he refused a grant of land made to him in 1504 on his arrival in Hispaniola: "But I came to get gold, not to till the soil like a peasant". Over a quarter of a century after the humiliating failure in Venezuela Las Casas still advised his king, in an unpublished letter which I was fortunate enough to discover in the castle-archive of Simancas, that the key to all the New World was the settlement of Hispaniola and the rest of the Indies with farmers. "If this were done, the king would have a great realm larger than Spain, which would make the king of France tremble; indeed, by securing the New World the king of Spain would hold the whole world within the grasp of his hand" [1].

Planned colonization remains to this day, however, the hope of almost every Spanish-speaking nation of the Americas. And Las Casas, by emphasizing the need for hard-working farmers to exploit the rich new lands rather than to exploit the Indians, anticipated the famous dictum of the Argentine statesman, Juan Bautista Alberti, "To govern is to populate".

---

[1] Letter to the king dated at Valladolid, February 20, 1559. Archivo General de Simancas, Sección de estado, legajo 138, fol. 360.

Closely allied to Las Casas' conviction that Spanish farmer-colonists could and should become the backbone of the conquest was another: the Indians could be converted to Christianity by peaceful means alone. This theory he successfully put into practice in the famous experiment which took place in Guatemala in the years following 1537. This experiment, like all of his work on behalf of the Indians, was solidly based on an idea, which Las Casas expounded at length in a treatise entitled *The Only Method of Attracting All People to the True Faith,* recently printed in Mexico for the first time [1].

The doctrine enunciated by Las Casas in this treatise, the first of his many polemical writings, was simple. He quoted, as did Pope Paul III in the bull "Sublimis Deus", the words of Christ, "go ye and teach all nations," and agreed with the pope that the American Indians were included. As the pope declared in Rome in that momentous pronouncement on June 9, 1537, at about the time that Las Casas was preaching the same doctrine in Guatemala:

> The sublime God so loved the human race that He not only created man in such wise that he might participate in the good that other creatures enjoy, but also endowed him with capacity to attain to the inaccessible and invisible Supreme Good and behold it face to face .... all are capable of receiving the doctrines of the faith ....
>
> We .... consider that the Indians are truly men and that they are not only capable of understanding the Catholic faith but, according to our information, they desire exceedingly to receive it. Desiring to provide ample remedy for these evils, we declare .... that, notwithstanding whatever may have been or

[1] This section is based upon the writer's introduction to this publication, entitled *Del único modo de atraer a todos los pueblos a la verdadera religión* (México, 1942).

> may be said to the contrary, the said Indians and all other people who may later be discovered by Christians, are by no means to be deprived of their liberty or the possession of their property, even though they be outside the faith of Jesus Christ; and that they may and should, freely and legitimately, enjoy their liberty and the possession of their property; nor should they be in any way enslaved; should the contrary happen it shall be null and of no effect.

Las Casas was much more specific than Pope Paul III in the application of this doctrine to the New World. For in the treatise he declared that wars against the Indians were unjust and tyrannical; hence the gold, silver, pearls, jewels and lands wrested from them were wrongfully gotten and must be restored. Not only was force unlawful to subdue and convert them; it was also unnecessary. Once the Indians accepted Christianity the next and inevitable step would be for them to acknowledge the king of Spain their sovereign.

Over and over again in this bulky treatise Las Casas emphasizes his point that "the way to bring into the bosom of the Christian faith and religion men who are outside the church must be a method which persuades their understanding, and which moves, exhorts and gently attracts the will." The only way to influence rational beings, he explains, is by the persuasion of their understanding, as Aristotle long ago pointed out. Moreover, following St. Augustine, faith depends upon belief which presupposes understanding. This emphasis upon understanding was later to bring Las Casas into public conflict with ecclesiastics who favored rapid and wholesale baptism of the natives, without too many questions asked or catechisms learned. The question became so hotly debated in the Indies that the crown referred it to Francisco de Vitoria, the renowned Dominican theologian at Salamanca.

LIBRARY OF MOUNT ST. MARY'S COLLEGE EMMITSBURG, MARYLAND

The Spanish colonists living in Guatemala were hugely amused by the ideas of this audacious friar. As one chronicler describes it, "even though the book was written in an elegant Latin," the colonists laughed at it and its author. The Lord had delivered this troublesome fellow into their hands, or so the colonists believed ,and their contempt took the form of urging Las Casas to put into practice his proposal to convert the Indians by peaceful means alone. They were very certain that even if Las Casas should escape with his life, his failure would be so resounding that they would henceforth be spared his annoying sermons.

The Spanish authorities provided an opportunity for the theory put forward by Las Casas to be tested, and may be said to have approached the problem in an experimental mood. But neither party to the controversy in Guatemala felt any doubt whatsoever of the outcome. Certainly Las Casas did not consider the proposal to be an experiment at all, but a demonstration of God's truth. Las Casas strongly emphasized the fact that Christ did not rest content with uttering His truths, but insisted on putting them into practice in the world about him. As one of Las Casas' favorite authorities, St. John Chrysostom, had declared:

> Men do not consider what we say but what we do — we may philosophize interminably, but if when the occasion arises we do not demonstrate with our actions the truth of what we have been saying, our words will have done more harm than good.

The moment for action in America had arrived and Las Casas selected for his demonstration the only land left unconquered in that region, the province of Tuzutlán — a mountainous, rainy, tropical country filled with fierce beasts, snakes, large monkeys, and, to boot, a land without salt. The natives living there were ferocious, barbarous, and impossible to subjugate — or at least so believed the Spaniards, for three times they had tried and as often had returned, "holding their heads", from this province which they forthwith named "Tierra de Guerra," "Land of War".

To this province and to this people Las Casas offered to go, to induce them voluntarily to become vassals of the king of Spain and pay him tribute according to their ability; to teach them and to preach the Christian faith, and all this without arms or soldiers. His only weapon would be the word of God and the "reasons of the Holy Gospel".

The two requests Las Casas made were modest, and Governor Alonso Maldonado speedily granted them: that the Indians won by peaceful methods should not be divided among the Spaniards but should depend directly upon the crown, with only moderate tribute to pay, and that for five years no Spaniards except Las Casas and his brother Dominicans should be allowed in the province, in order that secular Spaniards might not disturb the Indians or provoke scandal.

Having concluded this agreement with the governor, Las Casas and his companions — Friars Rodrigo de Andrada, Pedro de Angulo, and Luis Cáncer — spent several days praying, fasting, and undergoing other spiritual disciplines and mortifications. Then they carefully planned their approach and began by composing some ballads in the Indian language of the Tierra de Guerra. These ballads were virtually a history of Christianity, for they described the creation of the world and the fall of man, his exile from Paradise, and the life and miracles of Jesus Christ. Las Casas then sought and found Christian Indian merchants accustomed to trading in the Tierra de Guerra and patiently taught them by heart all the verses; and trained them, moreover, to sing them "in a pleasing manner".

At last, in August 1537, the Indians set out alone with their merchandise, to which Las Casas had added some Spanish trinkets, such as scissors, knives, mirrors, and bells, which had proved popular with the natives. The merchants went directly to the great chieftain of the tribes in the Tierra de Guerra, a warlike person, highly respected and feared by all. At the end of the day's trading one of the merchants called for a teplanastle, an Indian stringed instrument, and the group proceeded to sing all the verses they had learned. The novelty of the situation, the harmony of instrument and voices, and the new doctrine — especially the statement that the idols they worshipped were demons and that their human sacrifices were bad — excited great wonder and admiration among the Indians.

For the succeeding eight nights the merchants repeated their performance, gladly acceding to requests from the audience to sing some well-liked part over and over again. When the Indians wanted to know more, they were told that only the friars could instruct them. But what were friars? The merchants thereupon described them: men dressed in black and white robes, unmarried, their hair cut in a special fashion — men who wanted neither gold, feathers, nor precious stones, and who day and night sang the praises of their Lord before beautiful images in churches. Only these holy men — not even the great lords of Spain — could instruct the Indians, and the friars would come most willingly if invited. The chieftain was content with all that he had been told and sent his younger brother to ask the friars to come and teach them, instructing him, however, to observe secretly whether the friars behaved as well as the merchants alleged.

We may be sure that Las Casas and his associates passed some anxious days before their trusted merchants returned bringing with them the envoy and his retinue. They accepted joyfully the presents by the chieftain and, while the envoy was visiting the town, conferred and decided to send only one emissary, the Friar Luis Cáncer, a devoted and experienced missionary who knew Indian languages well. So the Indians, loaded down with Spanish trinkets, returned to their Tierra de Guerra, taking with them Friar Cáncer .On entering the chieftain's territory, he found triumphal floral arches raised and great fiestas prepared to welcome him. The chieftain himself received Cáncer with the greatest respect and veneration and ordered a church built at once. He was an interested spectator at the first mass celebrated there and was particularly impressed by the friar's vestments and cleanliness, for his own priests went about in filthy clothes, their hair matted with blood, and their temples were no more than sooty, dirty hovels. Assured by his brother that the friars really followed the customs described by the merchants, and his fear of armed invasion quieted by the news of Governor Maldonado's order, the chief decided to become a Christian and urged all his people to do likewise. He was the first to tear down and burn their ancient idols. Thus was won the first soul in the Tierra de Guerra, and the friars rejoiced in their victory, confident that they were at the beginning of a great spiritual harvest.

But the documents available tell a far different story — of a gradual decline from this high point of the conquest by peaceful means in Guatemala. The dramatic story of the eventual failure of the experiment in the "Land of True Peace," as the "Land of War" was officially christened after the initial success of the friars, cannot be told here. The conditions which alone would make such an effort ultimately successful — that is, Spanish colonists as selfless in their attitude as Las Casas — did not exist in the wilds of Guatemala any more than they had on the hot sands of Venezuela.

The original movers of the experiment carried on in the "Land of True Peace" never wavered in their conviction that all people — including Indians — could and should be brought to the faith by Christian, peaceful means, although many Spaniards continued to feel that "the voice of the gospel is heard only where the Indians have heard also the sound of firearms". But the ideal of peacefully bringing to the faith the natives of the marvelous New World discovered by the Spaniards lived on. The doctrine so carefully buttressed up by such a wealth of citations in *The Only Method of Attracting All People to the True Faith* was never wholly forgotten, despite the failure in the Land of True Peace. For other friars in other parts of the Spanish Empire in the New World were inspired by this treatise and by the Vera Paz experiment to follow the same ideal in their own territory.

The last experiment undertaken by Spaniards in the first half-century was also carried on because of the insistence of Las Casas that the Indians be protected. On November 20, 1542, Emperor Charles V cast aside the advice of some of his oldest and most important advisers and promulgated the famous New Laws, which revoked or limited the encomienda — the right of Spaniards to service and tribute from the Indians. The encomienda had been under continuous attack since the sermons of Montesinos. As we have seen, the colonization plan of 1521 was put forth by Las Casas as an alternative to the system of encomiendas. This plan failed but the disputes continued, although Las Casas for almost a decade was living quietly in a convent in Hispaniola and the battle was carried on by other Indian defenders.

The stoutest opponent of the encomienda system at the time was the Bishop of Santo Domingo, Sebastían Ramírez de Fuenleal, who was later to take part in the great battle of the New Laws in 1542. Now as President of the Audiencia of New Spain he recommended that royal officials be put in charge of the Indians and that conquistadores be given a regular pension. If the encomen-

Leyes y ordenanças nueuamẽte hechas por ſu Mageſtad/ pa la gouernacion de las Indias y buen tratamiento y conſeruacion de los Indios: que ſe han de guardar en el conſejo y audiẽcias reales q̃ en ellas reſiden: y por todos los otros gouernadores/ juezes y perſonas particulares dellas.

Con priuilegio imperial.

The New Laws of the Indies, 1542

deros complained that the land would therefore be depopulated and lost to the crown, Bishop Ramírez advised the crown on February 2, 1533, it could safely disregard such predictions, for Spaniards desirous of encomiendas had been making them since the conquest began.

The advice of this principal royal official in New Spain was not followed, and in 1536 the famous Law of Inheritance for two generations was passed, which permitted encomenderos to pass on their encomiendas as inheritances to their legitimate descendants or to their widows for one life. The law thus encouraged the hope that a permanent inheritance for the conquistadores and their families might soon be secured. Now voices were raised for grants in perpetuity, and even for a law which would hand over to the Spaniards, forever, civil and criminal jurisdiction over the Indians. Just at this juncture Las Casas arrived in Spain, fresh from the triumphs of peaceful preaching in the Land of True Peace in Guatemala, and determined that an even greater triumph must be achieved: the encomienda system itself must be destroyed.

So successful was Las Casas in portraying the cruelty of the Spaniards to the Indians and of the terrible results of the encomienda system that the *New Laws* were approved by Charles V. The climax was reached, for the encomenderos, by the laws taking Indians away from all royal officials and prelates, and prohibiting all future grants of Indians. As it was stipulated in Law No. 35, "Henceforth no encomienda is to be granted to anyone, and when the present holders of encomiendas die, their Indians will revert to the crown" [1].

The reaction of rage and astonishment among the conquistadores was instantaneous and inevitable. For by these laws the property of every encomendero was di-

---

[1] Henry Stevens, (ed.) *The New Laws of the Indies* (London ,1893), p. 16.

minished and the future of his family made insecure. All the most powerful officials, royal and ecclesiastical alike, were similarly disadvantaged. It was particularly galling to the colonial Spaniards who, as encomenderos, had developed secure and honored positions in the New World, that the Spaniards at home should have contrived these laws which, if enforced, would reduce the position and security of the very men who, in their own opinion, had contributed most to Spain's glory in the New World. The radical "Laws and Ordinances for the Government of the Indies and Good Treatment and Preservation of the Indians" led to a near revolt in Mexico, a serious rebellion in Peru, and provoked grave unrest throughout the empire.

Las Casas continued to press for more protection for the Indians throughout the remainder of 1543 and the early months of 1544. By spring he came to believe that their legal rights were so firmly established in Spain that his presence was no longer necessary at court. He must have known that representatives of conquistadores in Spain had hastily sent copies of the laws they hated to the New World and were grimly biding their time while waiting for the explosion they knew would come. Perhaps Las Casas expected this too, and wished to be in the thick of the fight in America.

At any rate Las Casas finally decided to accept the bishopric of Chiapa, in which lay the Land of True Peace. On Passion Sunday of 1544, this veteran of the Indies was consecrated bishop in the Church of St. Paul, in the "Very Noble and Very Loyal City" of Seville. Las Casas had been born there, and now it was from this same city that he set forth at seventy years of age to continue his labor for the Indians in Chiapa. He would be among friends, for in this bishopric his Dominican brothers were still succesfully putting into effect one of his great dreams, preaching the faith to Indians by peaceful means alone. Behind him lay, as he thought, his most spectacular victory over the forces of selfishness and ungodliness. The New Laws had been decreed, despite all the influence the conquistadores and their friends could muster against them, and these laws foreshadowed the eventual death of the encomienda system. The Dominican friar Bartolomé de Las Casas had set in motion as revolutionary a change in American society and in the administration of Spain's great empire overseas as his contemporary Nicolaus Copernicus had achieved in astronomical circles with his *De revolutionibus orbium coelestium,* printed in the same year as the New Laws.

No sooner had Las Casas started for America than there began a period of intense political activity to reverse the New Laws, culminating in a royal decision in 1545 to revoke the most protested ones, and Spaniards in the New World continued to enjoy the fruits of Indian labor.

The final decision of the crown to reverse itself not only terminated this experiment — it also terminated the period of experimentation in Indian affairs. No further attempt was made to change radically the basic laws and basic institutions that had been established in the fateful first half-century of the Spanish conquest of America.

Las Casas returned to Spain in 1547, renounced his bishopric and until his death in 1566 at the age of ninety-two devoted his days and nights to writing treatises on behalf of the Indians and in serving as their advocate before the king and Council of the Indies. During these twenty years he wrote most of his important works and elaborated his most significant doctrines. The general outlines of the life of Las Casas have long been known, particularly his attempts to intervene directly in the affairs of the New World, which ended largely in failure.

His ideas have been less well known, partly because they have been imbedded in ponderous treatises and partly because his actions provoked such strong opposition that men were in no mood to study and evaluate the thoughts of this impetuous, forthright and sometimes wrong-headed friar.

Even today the dust of controversy has not been fully laid, but it is at least possible to assess the real contribution made by Las Casas and it is my purpose to attempt to do so in the remaining two chapters, which will be devoted to the work of Bartolomé de Las Casas in the fields of political theory, history, and anthropology. In so doing, the full depth and significance can better be appreciated of that tremendous struggle which has given Spain's colonial effort its unique quality.

The struggle for justice was inevitable, given the nature of the Spaniards and the nature of the world. The story of the noise and the tumult raised by the irreconcilable groups as they attempted to shape the legislation and the government of the New World is not the whole story of Spain's action in America. Neither the martial conquest, for all its glamor and pageantry, nor the tenacious efforts of the defenders of the Indians to control and alter the conquest even while it rolled inexorably on is the whole story. But an understanding of the struggle for justice gives us, in my opinion, the most revealing picture of the conquest of America that we have.

This struggle for justice was a Quixotic attempt, we may say today, but Don Quixote was a true symbol of the Spanish nation in the epoch of Spain's glory. He was a man of ideals inspired by a passion to right the world's wrongs, and to this end hurled himself upon the world about him. Who can say that he was wrong? The poet and Hispanist Archer M. Huntington has well stated this age-old problem in words which may be applied appropriately to the conflict between conquistadores and justice-loving Spaniards:

Shall deeds of Caesar or Napoleon ring
More true than Don Quijote's vapouring?
Hath winged Pegasus more nobly trod
Than Rocinante stumbling up to God?

Chapter II

BARTOLOME DE LAS CASAS: POLITICAL THEORIST AND HISTORIAN

Bartolomé de Las Casas, who fought so stoutly for the Indians from his conversion in 1514 in Cuba until his death in 1566 in Spain, has usually been considered a noble humanitarian or a saintly fanatic, when harsher epithets have not been applied to him. Few of his friends or enemies have realized that under the fire and brimstone of his invective there existed a closely reasoned structure of political thought based upon the most fundamental concepts of medieval Europe.

The essence and significance of Las Casas' political theories cannot easily be distilled into a few neatly contrived generalizations. It is only by following through his numerous writings that one may understand the depth of his political thinking and the extent to which it underlay all his action on behalf of the Indians. Most of his writings, however, discussed the central problem with which all political theorists must grapple: What makes political dominion legitimate? More specifically, Las Casas demanded: What made Spain's rule in America legitimate?

The reason for his contemporary importance in the field of political theory was his dogged insistence through all his long career that Spain's title to the extensive and fabulous New World lands derived from the papal grant — from the donation made by Pope Alexander VI in 1493 which appointed King Ferdinand and Queen Isabella and their successors the "lords of the islands and mainland discovered or to be discovered with full, free, ample and absolute authority and jurisdiction" [1]. In spite of this, Las Casas maintained that the pope thereby entrusted the Spanish monarchs with only a missionary task and granted only such power and privilege as would enable them to achieve this limited objective. Failure to Christianize the Indians, insisted Las Casas, not merely jeopardized Spain's title but indeed invalidated it.

The Emperor Charles V, however, recognized no such interpretation and felt no qualms of conscience when he proudly announced on September 14, 1519, the incorporation of the New World in the territory under the royal crown of Castile in these words:

> By donation of the Holy Apostolic See and other just and legitimate titles we are Lord of the West Indies, the islands and mainland of the Ocean Sea already discovered or to be discovered [2].

Friar Montesinos, who had first questioned the validity of Spain's title to America in that Hispaniola sermon at Christmas time in 1511, had disturbed King Ferdinand sufficiently so that he ordered half a dozen theologians to work up replies for his benefit. These replies had satisfied Ferdinand but it was not only the king who had to satisfy himself about his just title. His loyal subjects did not fail to concern themselves as well with this problem, particularly after Las Casas began to insist that the papal concession alone justified the Spanish title and that this title was bestowed solely for the conversion of the Indians. As the conquest spread form the Caribbean islands to Mexico and Peru, to far-off Chile and the Philippines on

[1] For a résumé of past and present interpretations,see Silvio Zavala, *New Viewpoints on the Spanish Colonization of America* (Philadelphia, 1943), 17–28. The latest study is by Manuel Giménez Fernández, *Nuevas consideraciones sobre la historia, sentido y valor de las bulas alejandrinas de 1493 referentes a las Indias* (Sevilla, 1944).

[2] Ricardo Levene, *Introducción a la historia del derecho indiano* (Buenos Aires, 1924), 56–57.

the very periphery of the empire, there issued a flood of controversial treatises in both America and Spain which remind one of the bitter and learned polemics produced during the medieval investiture struggle. As in other times of confusion and violence, a great literary and philosophical outpouring resulted.

Scholars throughout Europe in the Renaissance were stimulated by the new vistas of the world being opened up by the voyagers to the east and to the west [1]. Spaniards were in the forefront of all these discussions and Spain became in the sixteenth century the home of the most illustrious scholastics since the thirteenth-century Thomas Aquinas. Robert Blakey has well described the ensuing development of political theory:

> There was no country in Europe in which politics, as a science, underwent a more general investigation and scrutiny .... than in Spain .... We find many elaborate treatises on the abstract principles of government, displaying freedom of enquiry and a degree of talent and learning which would do honor to any country .... The discovery of the American continent called forth new principles of administrative science and territorial right [2].

Of all the political questions discussed by the theorists, the legitimacy of Spain's title was clearly the most important and the most hotly disputed. It is easy to imagine the delight with which Spain's jealous rivals seized upon the writings of Las Casas on this subject, for his works were full of charges that the persistent mistreatment and despoilment of the Indians by the conquistadores imperiled Spain's title because it nullified the pope's intention. By the end of the sixteenth century, the Spanish nation was so sensitive to attacks on the justice of her rule in

[1] John L. Myres, "The influence of anthropology on the course of political science," *Report of the British Association for the Advancement of Science*, 1909 (London, 1910), 591, 592–94.

[2] Blakey, *History of Political Literature*, II (London, 1855), 365–70.

America that we find Antonio de Herrera, first important official historian of Spain's work in the Indies, undertaking his investigations about 1600 "so that foreign nations might know that these Catholic kings and their councilors have complied with the provisions of the papal bull, and have not simply despoiled those lands, as some say" [1]. This compulsion to affirm the justice of Spain's title continued on into the seventeenth century and later. For disputes concerning Spain's treatment of the Indians persisted throughout the three centuries of her rule. At the time Spain lost most of her American empire in the early decades of the nineteenth century, she was still defending herself from charges of cruelties inflicted against the Indians, and she was still protesting that her title to the New World rested upon unassailable foundations.

The political theories elaborated by Las Casas were to a large extent responsible for these doubts and protestations. These theories must be quarried out of the numerous treatises he composed, particularly the eight remarkable tracts for the times he published in Seville during the years 1552 and 1553 [2]. These weighty disquisitions are little read now, but they furnish undeniable evidence that Las Casas was not only a humanitarian zealot but also a scholar extraordinarily equipped with learning, ancient and medieval.

In these and other treatises, Las Casas' theory of the origin of government is elaborated and his thoughts on the power of the pope, as well as his theory of kingship and his views on the just title of Spain to the New World. Time does not permit a discussion of all these matters but it should be pointed out in connection with the origin

[1] Quoted by José Toribio Medina, *El descubrimiento del Océano Pacifico*, II (Santiago, 1913–1920), 516.

[2] For a listing of the titles of these works and detailed information on this whole subject, see the author's *Las teorías políticas de Bartolomé de Las Casas* (Buenos Aires, 1935.)

of government that Las Casas believed that all men originally were free, since individual liberty is a right conceded by God as an essential attribute of man. As for papal authority, he held that the pope has only voluntary jurisdiction over non-Christians, and cannot force them to accept Christianity, for this would be to follow Mahomet's method. The pope's power extends only to teaching pagans the falsity of their gods and the truth of Christ. Furthermore, the pope has no authority to deprive non-Christians of their lands or property, but his right and duty is limited to dividing among Christian kings the authority over the infidel world necessary to remove obstacles that infidels may place in the way of their conversion, and to preach the faith. In the case of the Indians, of course, the proper instruments are the kings of Castile.

Las Casas held firmly to the idea, however, that the Spanish kings to whom America was entrusted had the same attributes and responsibilities as medieval kings, who were but the rectors or administrators of public affairs. Thus all members of the kingdom are subjects not of the king's person but of the law.

Faced with his urgent problem of saving the Indians, Las Casas did not content himself with pious phrases but set up a long list of kingly obligations before which even a St. Louis might have quailed. Not even the injunctions of the League of Nations to its mandatory powers prescribed more saintly behavior.

Peace being a very important attribute of the Christian republic, the king must first of all deliver the Indians from the power of the Spaniards who war against them. He must then establish the fact that they are subjects of the crown and not to be oppressed or exploited. But the king's spiritual obligations are still heavier. He must ensure that the Christian faith be spread by mild and Christlike methods. He is to rule these Indian subjects by laws conforming to the natural and divine laws and adapted to the Christian faith. He is to break them of barbarous and irrational habits, and lead them to whatever is good. And finally, he is to ensure that not even their local chiefs oppress his people. Las Casas realizes that the kingly office is not a sinecure but is *grandíssimo y laboriosísimo.* Scriptural examples show that it goes hard with those who rule unjustly. Having elaborated this principle, Las Casas does not find it difficult to show that the system of encomiendas is tyrannical, and that the king of Spain and the Spaniards hold their lands and mines in the New World against the will of native kings. The Spaniards have not entered those kingdoms in the way that natural and human law require. The king ought, therefore, to restore the property to the rightful owners even though the encomenderos rebel and he has to kill some of them. Furthermore, the Spaniards who have robbed Indian sepulchres and treasure houses must return what they have stolen "to the penny". These forthright and logical conclusions demonstrate that the political theories of Las Casas on the monarchy were not academic speculations but were designed to have an immediate and practical application in the New World.

In fact, it may be said that every one of Las Casas' erudite though bellicose treatises had a most practical and immediate purpose in view. The one entitled *Some advice and regulations for confessors* was designed to withhold the sacraments of the church from all persons who held Indians or who did not properly compensate them for their labor. The hubbub raised in the Indies by these suggested rules was so great that Las Casas wrote another tract and presented it to the Council of the Indies to sustain his previous regulations. His enemies charged that he denied the jurisdiction of the kings of Castile in the New World when he asserted that everything the Spaniards had done in the Indies had been illegal, without the authority of the prince and against all justice. Las

Casas therefore wrote a treatise entitled *Thirty very juridical propositions* to justify his position.

Not having stilled his opponents with this treatise, he composed yet another, this time the one-hundred-and-sixty-page *Treatise concerning the imperial sovereignty and universal preëminence which the kings of Castile and León enjoy over the Indies,* a copy of which Thomas Jefferson owned at the time his books were sold to the Library of Congress. Reading this tremendous accumulation of legal citations, explosive argument, and close reasoning, we come to understand what Las Casas meant when he once said, "For forty-eight years I have been engaged in studying and inquiring into the law. I believe, if I am not mistaken, I have penetrated into the heart of this subject until I have arrived at the fundamental principles involved" [1].

This thorough knowledge of the law which Las Casas came to acquire must help to explain the fact that few of his contemporaries chose to meet him on the field of theory. Likewise, the freedom of speech permitted in sixteenth-century Spain and America explains why Las Casas was never hailed before courts as a traitor to his king and country. Strange as it may seem to us today, the crown encouraged its subjects to speak freely. As early as August 14, 1509, King Ferdinand ordered that "no official should prevent anyone from sending to the king or anyone else letters and other information which concern the welfare of the Indies," and in 1521 a standard instruction was issued which read:

> We order and emphatically maintain that now and henceforth at all times when each and every Royal Official and all other persons who are citizens and residents and inhabitants of the Indies, Islands and Tierra Firme of the Ocean Sea wish to write

[1] Antonio María Fabié, *Vida y escritos de Don Fray Bartolomé de Las Casas,* II (Madrid, 1879), 577–78.

> and give an account of everything that appears to be convenient to our service or if they wish to send messengers or come themselves, they shall be allowed to do these things and no one (including Captains, pilots and sailors) is to be permitted to place any restriction or hindrance or obstacle, whether directly or indirectly, under penalty of losing all favors, privileges, and positions granted by Us and loss of all property and under pain of Our displeasure [1].

Freedom of speech was, of course, subject to restrictions in certain fields such as religion. Nor was the press wholly free as the prohibition against some books, particularly after 1550, indicates. Some of the writings of the opponents of Las Casas, for example, were never allowed to be printed in the sixteenth century although he was able to distribute — all too freely in the opinion of some of his contemporaries — his published and unpublished tracts throughout Spain and the New World. On the other hand, those who challenged Las Casas wrote steadily and extensively to the crown against what they considered his exaggerations and falsehoods.

Emperor Charles V did not, however, always submit meekly to attacks on his right to rule America. In 1539 he abruptly and imperiously commanded the Dominicans of Salamanca to stop such discussions forthwith and to collect all sermons and other dissertations that the monks had prepared on this delicate subject, so that they might be duly studied. The Prior was to make sure that no further statements be made or printed without express royal permission. It was this incident which probably was responsible for the exclamation of Samuel Johnson: "I love the University of Salamanca; for when the Spaniards were in doubt as to the lawfulness of their

[1] For exact citation to this order and for other information on the subject, see the writer's "Free speech in sixteenth-century America", *Hispanic American Historical Review*, XXVI (1946), 135–49.

conquering America, the University of Salamanca gave it as their opinion that it was not lawful". Boswell tells us that "he spoke this with great emotion" [1].

Doubts did not cease at the king's order, however, and the disputes were stopped only temporarily. In particular Las Casas was not quieted for he adopted an independent attitude even toward his king, where the welfare of the Indians was involved. He had once declared publicly to the king's face, while reciting the iniquities practiced by Spaniards in the Indies:

> I am certain that I am rendering Your Majesty one of the greatest services that a vassal may make to his Prince, and I do this not because I desire any kind of reward or prize, because I am not doing this to serve Your Majesty, since it is certain (speaking with all respect and reverence due such a great king and lord) that I would not move from this spot to another spot to serve Your Majesty, except for the fidelity I owe you as a subject, unless I thought and believed that I was thereby making a great sacrifice to God [2].

It was precisely in this spirit that Las Casas set forth his theories concerning the right of Spain to rule the vast territories of America.

He disposes summarily of the illegal and unjust titles to the New World which some persons have brought forward. To those who suggest that Spain's proximity to the Indies gives her a superior right, Las Casas points out that Portugal really lies closer to the New World. To those who urge the greater wisdom and understanding of Spaniards as justifying their lordship over the Indians, he replies that many other nations are wiser and of greater genius than Spain — witness the Greeks, the Africans, and the Asians. To those who cite the opinion of Ostiensis to the effect that all infidels are unworthy of exercising

---

[1] James Boswell, *The Life of Samuel Johnson,* I (London, 1924), 302.

[2] Las Casas, *Historia de las Indias,* III : 322.

jurisdiction, he retorts that these persons do not really understand the true meaning of Ostiensis, as he had already proved in detail in a Latin treatise. As for those who establish Spain's title because Indians are idolatrous, or commit unnatural crimes, they do not seem to realize that the Indians live for the most part an orderly, political life in towns, and in some respects are superior to Spaniards.

Finally, the worst justification of all is that advanced by those who justify Spain's title by her mere superiority in arms, which is "an absurd, nefarious argument unworthy of being advanced by Christian and reasonable men". As Las Casas declared in replying to one of his most able critics, Dr. Juan Ginés de Sepúlveda:

> The Doctor (Sepúlveda) founds these rights upon our superiority in arms, and upon our having more bodily strength than the Indians. This is simply to place our kings in the position of tyrants. The right of those kings rests upon their extension of the gospel in the New World, and their good government of the Indian nations. These duties they would be bound to fulfill even at their own expense; much more so considering the treasures they have received from the Indies. To deny this doctrine is to flatter and deceive our monarchs, and to put their salvation in peril. The Doctor perverts the natural order of things, making the means the end, and what is accessary the principal .... He who is ignorant of this, small is his knowledge, and he who denies it is no more of a Christian than Mahomet was. .... To this end (to prevent the total perdition of the Indies) I direct all my efforts, not, as the Doctor would make out, to shut the gates of justification and annul the sovereignty of the kings of Castile; but I shut the gate upon false claims made on their behalf, and I open the gates to those claims of sovereignty which are founded upon law, which are solid, strong, truly Catholic and truly Christian [1].

[1] Translation by Arthur Helps, *The Spanish Conquest in America*, IV (London, 1855), 577–78. For the original Spanish, see Las Casas, *Colección de tratados, 1552–1553* (Buenos Aires, 1924), 230.

A complete exposition of Las Casas' political theories would require much more spare than is presently available, but enough has been said to demonstrate that he was neither a closet theologian nor merely a burning humanitarian but almost incidentally a political theorist of real stature in a century of great Spanish political thinkers.

His lasting concern of course was to move the men of his time to defend the Indians with the same passion that he felt. The strength of his feeling and the quality of his mind enabled him to apply medieval theories to the problems raised by the discovery of America in such an arresting way that his contemporaries were obliged to listen to him. His doctrines did not wholly triumph, but he raised such doubts in the minds of his fellow men that the Town Council of Mexico City commissioned the writing of treatises to disprove and discredit his theories, and Viceroy Francisco de Toledo initiated in Peru a wholesale investigation into Inca rule in an effort to demonstrate its injustice, and thereby to establish the justice of Spanish rule [1]. The galaxy of laws designed to protect the Indians were to a considerable extent fashioned because of his insistence that the just and only true title of Spain depended upon bringing the Indians to Christianity.

Two incidents occurred after Viceroy Toledo's investigations in Peru which show that scruples concerning the justice of Spanish rule were raised not only by theologians, jurists, historians and other erudite persons, but by more ordinary folk as well. When the explorer and administrator Pedro Sarmiento de Gamboa went on his ill-fated expedition to the Strait of Magellan in 1581–1582, one of his sea captains, Diego Flores, exclaimed petulantly that "he didn't see what title the king had to the Indies any-

[1] For a detailed description of this, see the writer's article on this subject, "Francisco de Toledo and the just titles of Spain to the Inca empire", *The Americas*, III (Washington, 1946), 3–19.

way". Sarmiento was properly distressed and proceeded to lecture Flores on all the titles the king held. But none of these reasons persuaded the captain until Sarmiento showed him a copy of the bull of Alexander VI and sternly warned him that anyone who contradicted this title contradicted the power of the pope, and soiled the royal conscience. Only then did Flores fall silent [1].

The second incident involved the last will and testament of that gallant conquistador Mancio Serra, who was famous throughout Peru for having been awarded the celebrated golden image of the sun which had been the chief ornament of the Temple of the Sun in Cuzco, and was even more famous for having promptly lost it in a card game. In 1589 Serra, now the oldest living conquistador, was on his deathbed, and, wishing to ease his conscience, solemnly swore to the following deposition before a notary public:

> That the Incas had ruled so wisely that in all their realms there was not a single thief, vicious or lazy man, or adulterous woman; that immoral persons were not countenanced; that every man had an honest and profitable occupation; that the mountains, mines, and lands were all so administered that everyone had enough; that the Incas were obeyed and respected by their subjects and considered very capable rulers [2].

Ironically enough, the Viceroy Toledo seems to have agreed with Serra to some extent for the many laws and administrative regulations he worked out for the Indians — which won for him the name of "Solon of Peru" — were based on the system developed centuries before by the Incas.

For those of us reared in the English tradition, the great attention paid by Spaniards to the legal basis of

[1] *Ibid.*, pp. 17–18.
[2] *Ibid.*, p. 18.

their rule may seem curious and bizarre. Certainly, few instances may be discovered in our own colonial history of English preoccupation with such matters. Roger Williams, in Rhode Island, did compose a manuscript in which he questioned the right of Plymouth to Indian lands unless by direct purchase in a voluntary sale, but after the chief men and ministers of Boston condemned these "errors and presumptions in which treason might lurk" he wrote "very submissively" to Governor Winthrop offering to burn part or all of the manuscript [1]. To Spaniards, however, the basis for the just title by which their king ruled the Indies was a palpitating question throughout most of the sixteenth century. It was certainly uppermost in the mind of Las Casas throughout his life, as his last will and testament shows. In this spirited and touching document, drawn up on March 17, 1564, when Las Casas was ninety years of age, he once more excoriated his countrymen for their cruelty and injustice to the Indians, referred to the natives as "the owners and proprietors of those lands and kingdoms," and stated his conviction that on account of "those impious and ignominious actions of Spaniards, so unjust, tyrannical and barbarous, God some day will vent His fury and anger against Spain [2].

But Las Casas was not content, for he wanted his king to recognize these truths, too, and the next year at the age of ninety-one prepared a large treatise in Latin entitled *De Thesauris* and, according to a note on the manuscript, now in the John Carter Brown Library, planned to offer it to the king as if he were "bestowing upon him a great inheritance" [3]. While he was awaiting the opportune moment to deliver this treatise to Philip II, a brother

---

[1] James Ernst, *Roger Williams* (New York, 1932), 80, 101–3, 130.

[2] Antonio María Fabié, *Vida y escritos de fray Bartolomé de las Casas*, I (Madrid, 1879), 235.

[3] See the writer's *Cuerpo de documentos del siglo XVI* (México, 1943), 27, 324.

Dominican came to him with certain doubts cencerning the conquest of Peru. Las Casas felt obliged to respond and forthwith composed another treatise *Solution of the Twelve Doubts,* and presented both treatises to Philip II as a sort of special will and codicil, with the request that Philip convoke a meeting of jurists and theologians to study the matter. Both these lengthy treatises were read in their entirety before the full Council of the Indies and a distinguished group of royal advisers on American affairs shortly before Las Casas died.

Las Casas did not limit his efforts to protecting the Indians by insisting that the royal title be established on what he considered a just basis. He was also much concerned to make sure that posterity should view the struggles of his time in the same light as he did. To this end he composed a large *History of the Indies* in the same spirit as, in his will, he ordered his papers to be organized so that, "if in the years to come God decided to destroy Spain on account of her misdeeds in the New World" [1]. everyone who read his history or consulted his documents would understand the reasons therefor. And so horrendous a story did he tell that he forbade the general reading of the history for forty years. In his letter of 1559 to the rector and chapter of the San Gregorio monastery in Valladolid, with whom he deposited the manuscript, he says:

> And when those forty years have passed, if they shall see that it is well for the good of the Indians and of Spain, they may command that it be printed for the glory of God and especially for the showing forth of the truth [2].

Note that Las Casas places the good of the Indians before the good of Spain! He does not consider these two

[1] Fabié, *op. cit.*, I : 237.
[2] Las Casas, *Historia de las Indias,* I : 1.

objectives incompatible, for in the eight reasons he set forth in the prologue to explain the writing of the work he makes clear that he has aimed "to profit Spain by revealing the truth concerning the Indies," as well as to save the good name of the king of Spain and "to deliver his nation from the error of thinking that the Indians were not rational beings" [1].

He believed himself better qualified than anyone else to write the almost incredible story of Spanish action in America, and the *History of the Indies* goes far to substantiate this claim. No Spaniard had a more direct connection with the events and the personalities of those glorious and tragic years. Through his father and his uncle, who had accompanied Columbus on his second voyage, Las Casas had learned much of the first decade of the conquest. He himself first set foot on the New World soil in 1502. For the next sixty-four years he participated successively as priest, conquistador, and encomendero in the Caribbean islands, reformer at the court in Spain, colonizer in Venezuela, friar in Hispaniola, obstructor of wars he considered unjust against the Indians of Nicaragua, fighter for justice in bitter debates among the ecclesiastics in Mexico, promotor of the plan to conquer and Christianize Guatemalan Indians by peaceful means alone, successful agitator before Emperor Charles V on behalf of the New Laws, and Bishop of Chiapa. Upon his final return to Spain in 1547 at the age of seventy-three, he served as attorney-at-large for the Indians during the last two decades of his turbulent life.

Since his arrival in Hispaniola as a young man of twenty-eight, he had known the great men who were carving out an empire for themselves and for Spain, from Columbus and his sons to Fernando Cortés, Francisco Pizarro, Bernal Díaz del Castillo and a host of other conquistadores. For their part, many of the Spanish

[1] *Ibid.*, I : 17–18.

officials, ecclesiastics, and conquistadores had come to know, and to dislike, this friar who so boldly denounced their actions. He had also argued on behalf of the Indians before Spanish kings and their Council of the Indies, as well as at the frequent special meetings held to discuss Indian problems. It is safe to say that no one had enjoyed as intimate a connection with American affairs as Las Casas.

Yet the volumes he so devotedly compiled in his old age which describe the history of America up to 1520 have never been wholly accepted as true history, and a sharp controversy has always existed on his merits as a historian. The defects of the *History of the Indies* are easy to point out. It is badly organized, the narrative weaves in and out to the confusion of the reader and sometimes stops entirely while irrelevant chapters are introduced. Las Casas could, and sometimes did, write succinctly, even brilliantly. But often his prose wallows in a sea of quotations and references. The history, too, is a well-stuffed work and, like the volume of his famous contemporary Jean Bodin, entitled *Method for the Easy Understanding of History,* may be described as a "confused and often muddied stream on whose surface float strange spars of knowledge" [1].

The most serious charge against Las Casas, not yet established, is that he falsified documents to prove his points — an accusation leveled by the Argentine historian Rómulo D. Carbia who recently died before providing the necessary evidence [2]. It is likely that the charge will never be proved, for most historians — whether they

[1] John L. Brown, *The Methodus ad facilem historiarum cognitionem of Jean Bodin: a critical study* (Washington, 1939), 85.

[2] "La supercheria en la historia del descubrimiento de América," *Humanidades,* XX (La Plata, 1930), 169–184. Carbia wrote a number of articles on this topic, most of which are cited in his *La crónica oficial de las Indias Occidentales* (Buenos Aires, 1940). For a penetrating criticism of Carbia's attitude, see Samuel Eliot Morison, *Admiral of the Ocean Sea,* I (Boston, 1942), 20, 23, 206 and vol. II : 289.

like Las Casas or not — generally concede his honesty, which, in fact, is so apparent in every chapter that his bias is public and unmistakable. Las Casas passionately believed that the early years of Spanish dominion constitute one of the darkest pages in the annals of mankind — that his countrymen, carried away by blind lust for gold, displayed the most wanton and fiendish barbarity toward the meek and defenseless natives whom they were supposed to bring to a knowledge of Christ. His indignation boils over time and time again as he recounts some atrocious deed committed against the Indians.

The virtues of the *History of the Indies* are as obvious as its defects. Las Casas was there, he had witnessed many of the events he described or had talked with the principal actors, and he had assiduously collected the written sources. Thus his work has an intimacy and authority enjoyed by no other history of the time.

Moreover, he showed critical ability in the handling of his sources, and often exhibited a healthy skepticism. Though he naturally describes at length his own part in the struggles on behalf of the Indians, he does not fail to give credit to many other persons and to cite their good work.

The struggle to save the Indians is uppermost in his mind, but much other valuable information on the great enterprise of the Indies may be found here. The danger and the wonder of the voyage to the New World, the grievous inflation of the times — in forty years the price of equipping expeditions had gone up 300 per cent — the smallpox epidemic, the plague of ants, the first manufacture of sugar in America, the question whether syphilis originated in the Old World or the New — all these and many other matters are discussed and described by Las Casas.

He had a truly elephantine memory, too, to have been able to recollect so many details of events long past.

Writing about 1560, he recalled the triumph he had won back in 1520 when Emperor Charles granted him permission to enter upon his plan to colonize in Venezuela and decided, with the concurrence of the Council of the Council of the Indies, "that the Indians were free men, ought to be treated as such and induced to accept Christianity by the methods Christ had established". It had been a notable victory and as Las Casas set it all down in his history, he still savoured the taste of triumph and told again the joke he and Cardinal Adrian had cracked in Latin over the outcome [1]. Who among us could remember the multitude of details such as Las Casas crowded into his history — even those relating to our victories — if they had occurred to us forty years ago?

Most important of all, perhaps, for students today is the quantity and quality of manuscript material available to him for writing the history. Las Casas was as earnest as every graduate student is supposed to be in searching out original sources of information. The greatest single document on the discovery, the journal kept by Columbus as he proceeded westward on his first voyage, was preserved for the world because Las Casas transcribed it for use in writing his history. He also had available, and utilized in his text, letters written by Columbus and by other great actors in the drama of the discovery of America; several important treatises were saved because Las Casas embedded them in his history.

Comparison with other important historians of the time will help to show the advantages Las Casas enjoyed.

Bernal Díaz, the foot soldier of Cortés whose *True History of the Conquest of New Spain* constitutes one of the classics of the Americas, based it primarily upon his own recollections. Francisco López de Gómara never saw America and relied largely upon documents of Cortés. Gonzalo Fernández de Oviedo used both docu-

[1] Las Casas, *Historia de las Indias*, III : 343.

ments and his own experience overseas ,but his work was in both respects inferior to that of Las Casas. Peter Martyr, the Italian humanist who hung around the Spanish court picking up news of America as it reached Spain, never saw the New World. Las Casas was in fact, then, as he himself asserted, better equipped with information and experience than any other writer of his time. He appreciated, moreover, the importance of his sources and the magnitude of the story they told. "It is certain," he once exclaimed,

> that in order to do justice to the grandeur and the dignity of the affairs of the Indies, which God has placed in the hands of the kings of Castile, the eloquence of Demosthenes would be needed, and to describe them the skill of Cicero [1].

The composition of this history became the principal concern of Las Casas during the last fifteen or twenty years of his life, when he had the time and quiet necessary for the handling of the many sources upon which it rested. He did not achieve his original intention of telling the story to 1550; the manuscript that has come down to us reaches only to the year 1520.

In one essential respect Las Casas was more fortunate than many historians. He had no publication problem, since he did not desire that his work be published, at least until forty years after his death, as he charged his Dominican brothers in leaving them his manuscript. It was actually not printed for over three hundred years. This is not the place to detail the political and other maneuvers which delayed the publication. The decision to print the work at long last, however, was probably influenced by the determined action of an American, the Cuban historian José Antonio Saco. The Royal Academy of History in Madrid had approved in the years 1817–1819

---

[1] *Ibid.*, I : 539.

the issuance of Las Casas' work as the first in a series of histories of America under the aegis of the Academy [1].

Ferdinand VII, once he had lost most of his dominions in America by the revolutions that began about 1810, had ordered a thorough investigation in Spanish archives so that all the important material on the conquest might be brought together, in order to justify Spain's conduct and to demonstrate to the world the lack of substance in the charge that her New World realms had broken away because of her bad treatment of them. In 1832 the Academy decided against publication after all and there the matter rested until Saco undertook to induce the Academy to reverse this decision. He asserted, in a vigorous article published in 1865 in a Madrid review, that the real reasons for keeping the *History of the Indies* out of print were political and of such a nature that "no lover of the glories of Spain could admit them," nor could he as an American. And he urged that the Academy decide to publish Las Casas after all in these words:

> If the *History* contains some errors, the Academy can easily correct them because it possesses a great collection of material on America and very distinguished members who could undertake this honorable task. If exaggerations are to be found in the work, they can easily be scaled down so that the deeds stand out in their true value. If the ideas are incoherent and the style heavy, the history would be at least available for those curious and persistent enough to undertake its reading; but none of these motives nor any others that might be alleged are sufficient to permit that there remains buried in the dust of a library the story of the extraordinary events and the great historical and moral truths described by the pen of one of the men who most honor Spain and humanity [2].

---

[1] On the Academy's various actions,see Cesáreo Fernández Duro's report in the *Boletin de la Real Academia de Historia*, XLII (1903), 5–59.

[2] Saco's article "La Historia de las Indias por Fray Bartolomé de las Casas, y

Saco's campaign was successful; at least the history was finally published in Madrid in 1875. The editor did not attempt to evaluate the work, but contented himself with quoting George Ticknor's statement:

> It is a great repository .... without which the history of the earliest period of Spanish settlements in America cannot even now be properly written [1].

Even then the original manuscript was not reproduced and the two subsequent editions were based on the 1875 version with no real introduction or adequate notes. The need for a critical edition of the manuscript in Las Casas' hand was recognized, however, and the XXVI Congress of Americanists in 1935 formally resolved that it be brought out [2]. Now, due to the energy and imagination of a Mexican publisher, and to the collaboration of a Spanish refugee scholar with a North American historian, such an edition is to be issued in America, whose lands and peoples Las Casas loved so well.

The appearance of this new edition will not stop the great debate on Las Casas' merits as a historian. To a large extent the popular conception of his writing is derived from his propaganda tract, not really history at all, entitled *Very Brief Account of the Destruction of the Indies,* which was presented in 1542 to Charles V in an attempt, successful for a time, to persuade the Emperor to decree the eventual abolition of the encomienda system. This bitter denunciation of Spanish treatment of the Indians caused oceans of words to flow in the sixteenth and succeeding centuries, including our own. This

---

la Real Academia de la Historia de Madrid" first appeared in the *Revista hispona-americana de Madrid* on February 12, 1865. Later he republished it in his *Historia de la esclavitud de la raza africana en el mundo nuevo y en especial en los paises américo-hispanos,* tomo 1 (Barcelona 1869), Apéndices, pp. 373–80. The latter version is the one used here.

[1] *History of Spanish Literature,* II (Boston, 1872), 46.

[2] Manuel Ballesteros Gaibrois, "XXVI Congreso Internacional de Americanistas", *Tierra firme,* I (Madrid, 1935), 133–38.

DEN

SPIEGHEL

Vande Spaensche Tyrannie beeldelijcken af-
gemaelt / leest breederen in-hout door het schrijven van den E. Bisschop
van Chiapa in nieu Spaengien / ghenaemt Don Fray Bartholome de
las Casas, van S. Dominicus Orden / aen den grootmach-
tigen Coninck van Spaengien Philips de tweede.

Ghedruckt tot Amstelredam by Cornelis Claesz. 1609.

One of the famous De Bry illustrations from a Dutch translation of the *Very Brief Account of the Destruction of the Indies.*

bloody description of the Spanish conquest, translated into all the principal European languages and illustrated with gruesome pictures, served as the choicest weapon of anti-Spanish propagandists everywhere. Even today it seems to have a Lorelei-like attraction for Hispanophiles who wish to combat the black legend of Spanish cruelty in America, and the revisionists quote Las Casas so frequently in their attacks on his writings that they help spread ever more widely his accusations [1].

At once there sprang up persons to challenge Las Casas' statistics — for he claimed some fifteen or twenty millions of Indians had perished — and to complain that he gave a most unbalanced picture of Spanish deeds in the New World in the first half-century after Columbus. His vehemence in 1542 has been matched by the vehemence of other Spaniards who have been denouncing him these four hundred years.

It is not possible to present here an essay on the comparative cruelty of Europeans in America which would do justice to this large theme [2]. No one today would defend the statistics Las Casas gave, but few would deny that there was considerable truth in his main charges. One Mexican writer, who has devoted himself to analyzing the *Very Brief Account*, concludes that the detractors of Las Casas have shrewdly exploited his numerical errors without ever disproving his essential truths [3].

Las Casas was, of course, not alone in charging his countrymen with cruelty. The secret investigation against Viceroy Antonio de Mendoza contained this accusation:

After the capture of the hill of Mixton, many of

[1] One of the best and most recent examples of this is Rómulo D. Carbia's *Historia de la leyenda negra hispanoamericana* (Buenos Aires, 1943).

[2] Some bibliographical assistance for such a study will be found in the writer's "Dos palabras on Antonio de Ulloa and the Noticias Secretas", *Hispanic American Historical Review*, XVI (1936), 479–514.

[3] Agustín Rivera y Sanromán, *Principios criticos sobre el virreinato de la Nueva España: sobre la revolución de independencia*, I (Lagos, 1884), 262–75.

> the Indians taken in the conquest of the said hill were put to death in his presence and by his orders. Some were placed in line and blown into bits by cannon fire; others were torn to pieces by dogs; and others were given to Negroes to be put to death, and these killed them with knife thrusts, while others were hung. Again, at other places, Indians were thrown to the dogs in his presence [1].

Friar Motolinía, certainly no friend of Las Casas and author of one of the bitterest and most sarcastic letters ever written against him, stated in the *History of the Indians of New Spain* that "countless" natives were destroyed in labor at the mines, that service in the mines of Oaxyecac was so destructive that for half a league around it the Spaniards could not walk except on dead men or bones, and that so many birds came to scavenge that they darkened the sky [2]. The royal official Alonso de Zurita stated that he had heard many Spaniards say that in Popayán province the bones of dead Indians were so thick along the roads that one could never lose the way [3]. Governor Francisco de Castañeda in Nicaragua reported that Spaniards on horseback hunted down Indians and lanced them, including women and children, at the slightest provocation or with no provocation whatsoever [4].

Some of the most telling descriptions of Spanish cruelty were embedded in royal orders, so much so that the seventeenth-century jurist Solórzano was ordered to remove from the manuscript of his *Politica Indiana* some of the royal orders on mistreatment of Indians to prevent notice of these things reaching foreigners [5]. Anyone who

---

[1] Arthur S. Aiton, "The secret *visita* against Viceroy Mendoza," *New Spain and the Anglo-American West*, I (Los Angeles, 1932), 29.

[2] Motolinía, *Historia de los indios de la Nueva España* (Barcelona, 1914), 17–19. Ed. by Daniel Sánchez García.

[3] *Documentos inéditos de América*, II : 113, 117, 118–19.

[4] León Fernández, *Colección de documentos para la historia de Costa Rica*, VI (San José, 1881–1907), 206–207.

[5] Archivo General de Simancas, Estado 2660. *Consulta* of March 12, 1638.

reads widely in the chronicles and reports left by Spaniards will find information supporting and supplementing many of the accusations made by Las Casas in 1542.

Nevertheless, the *Very Brief Account* establishes Las Casas as a polemical writer, not as a historian. His claim to the title of historian must rest upon the *History of the Indies*. For those who prefer "objective" history, the passion which he injected into every page of it will always mar his work. Others will agree with the late Ramón Iglesia, a perspicacious scholar and certainly no blind follower of Las Casas, that:

> True history, that which has vigor and reality, ... is polemical history, partial, passionate, and tendentious. The true history which interests the historiographer, who always tries to get as close as possible to the events themselves .... is history written to prove something [1].

If one wishes, for contrast, to see how another great Spaniard described, without passion, the events in which he participated, read the famous letters written by the conquistador Cortés to inform his king of the great things accomplished in America, and the progress of the conquest. As Iglesia has remarked, Cortés displayed some sorrow over the death of one of his valuable horses, but related calmly that his men had killed over five hundred of the "principal and most valiant Indians," and that he had permitted his native allies to chop off pieces of the enemy dead for their evening meal. Cortés used an indulgent tone in describing these actions, "such as a grandfather would employ toward the pranks of his lively grandson" [2].

The final determination of the real value of the *His-*

---

[1] *Estudios de historiografía de la Nueva España.* Con una introducción de Ramón Iglesia (Mécixo, 1945), 10.

[2] Ramón Iglesia, *Cronistas e historiadores de la conquista de México* (México, 1942), 47–48.

tory of the Indies is still to come, but it will be more easily reached when the critical edition based on the original manuscript appears. Whatever may be the errors, inconsistencies, and exaggerations discovered by scholars, it is likely that most students will agree with Samuel Eliot Morison, the latest historian to analyze carefully the sources on the discovery who characterized the *History of the Indies* as "a great and noble history .... the one book on the discovery of America that I should wish to preserve if all others were destroyed" [1]. It is, in truth, a passionate and an indispensable record of the first coming of the white man to America, which recreates for us today the heat and the bitter struggles of those far-off wondrous days. And it is no small tribute to the conviction and the energy of Las Casas that he was able to disturb the conscience of Spain with his political theories and to provide such a valuable history that no one can ignore it in studying the conquest of America. He was most versatile, as well, for the descriptions of the culture of the Indians which he compiled in the course of defending them, resulted in his producing a most comprehensive picture of their civilization. He was, indeed, one of the first American anthropologists as will be described in the following chapter.

---

[1] Samuel Eliot Morison, *Admiral of the Ocean Sea*, I (Boston, 1942), 68, 70–71.

Chapter III

BARTOLOMÉ DE LAS CASAS: ANTHROPOLOGIST

To call Bartolomé de Las Casas an anthropologist may seem to some not only inaccurate but presumptuous as well. It is true that he was an anthropologist only incidentally, for he was primarily a man of action determined to influence the course of events in America. It was to protect the Indians from cruel and devastating wars of conquest against them, and to defend them from the charge that they were slaves according to Aristotle's theory that certain classes of human beings are inherently slaves, that Las Casas became a student of Indian culture. Certainly he did not possess all the skills required of an anthropologist today. But his attempt to describe the cultures of the American Indians, in the course of his defense of the natives, resulted in his producing a most comprehensive picture of their civilization. His works constitute even today one of the indispensable sources on the native people encountered during the course of what Spaniards of that time believed to be the Eighth Wonder of the World — the discovery of America.

It is not surprising, however, that his contribution as an anthropologist has not yet been fully recognized. His known character as an ardent defender of the Indians has made many students suspect, often quite rightly, that he failed to give all the evidence, and his well-known exaggeration of the number of Indians killed by Spaniards has led others to reject everything he said about the Indians. His right to be called an anthropologist rests, it seems to me, upon his approach to the study of cultures so alien to his own. He did not automatically assume that the Indians should be measured by a Spanish yardstick but on the contrary tried to understand the importance of their customs and beliefs within the framework of their own culture. He looked at all peoples, the ancient Greeks and sixteenth-century Spaniards as well as the newly discovered New World natives, as human beings in different stages of development from rude beginnings to a higher stage of culture. To set forth both the way in which Las Casas developed this theme, and the use he made of the vast amount of material he had patiently gathered on various aspects of Indian life is the purpose of this chapter.

The significance of the attitude Las Casas developed toward the Indians must, first of all, be judged and understood against the standards and attitudes of his contemporaries. Almost every Spaniard who went to America in the early years of the conquest viewed the recently discovered natives with a keen interest and held strong views concerning their true nature. Columbus, returned from his first voyage and intent on presenting a rosy-tinted picture of America to the Crown, declared that the natives he had encountered were all ready for Christianity and that they all had the same customs and all spoke the same language [1]. This naive and simple description could not, of course, stand and there soon developed an astonishing variety of information on and conjecture about the past, present, and future of the Indians [2].

Many of the conquistadores and other secular Spaniards displayed the same attitude as the gentleman who,

---

[1] Martín Fernández de Navarrete; *Colección de los viajes y descubrimientos que hicieron por mar los españoles desde fines del siglo XV*. Tomo II (Paris, 1825), 385. The statement occurs in a letter written by Columbus, addressed to the Treasurer of Spain, on his return from the first voyage.

[2] The writer has collected a quantity of information on this topic in *The first social experiments in America* (Cambridge, 1935), 74–81.

about 1900, spent some time among wild tribes in a foreign land and wrote a book about them on his return to civilization. One chapter was headed "Customs and Manners", and consisted of these words: "Customs, beastly; manners, none" [1]. Some curious ideas were held concerning the origin of these newly discovered people and more than one grave Spanish historian considered them descendants of the lost tribes of Israel and at least one sixteenth-century writer was firmly convinced that Quetzalcóatl, the Indian god who appears in the pre-conquest history of Mexico as a great civilizer, was in reality Thomas Aquinas [2]. Quetzalcóatl seems to have fascinated other writers too, for an eminent nineteenth-century anthropologist, Edward Tylor, who also held the theory that the lost tribes of Israel had somehow wandered to Mexico, believed as firmly that the Mexican god was a real man and even hinted that he may have been an Irishman [3].

It was the friars, looking for souls to win, rather than the conquistadores, whose preoccupations were more mundane, who first began to study Indian customs and languages. The missionaries needed to know the names and attributes of Indian gods, the sacrifices made to them, and as much as possible of the mentality of the Indians in order to lead them away from their pagan rites and toward Christianity. One may say that the founder of American anthropology was Friar Ramón Pane, [4] who accompanied Columbus on his second voyage for the express purpose

[1] Washington Matthews, "The study of ethics among the lower races," *Journal of American folklore*, XII (1899), 1.

[2] *Estudios en la historiografía de la Nueva España* (México, 1945), 66–70. Introduction by Ramón Iglesia.

[3] Robert R. Marett, *Tylor* (New York, 1936), 36.

[4] The available information on Pane has been collected by Edward G. Bourne in "Columbus, Ramon Pane and the beginnings of American anthropology", *Proceedings of the American Antiquarian Society* (April, 1906) and by Robert Streit in "Fr. Ramon Pane, der erste Etnograph Amerikas," *Zeitschrift für Missionswissenschaft*, band 10 (Münster i. W., 1920).

of observing the natives and reporting on their ways.

The crown encouraged the ecclesiastics throughout the sixteenth century to study the Indians [1] and numerous volumes on Indian language and customs were in fact compiled by friars [2]. The most significant contributions were probably made by the Franciscan Bernardino de Sahagún [3], the first great anthropologist in America, and by Bishop Diego de Landa whose "Account of the. Indians of Yucatan" has remained a classic to this day [4]. No individual, however, wrote more about the Indians in the sixteenth century than Las Casas, or attempted to present such a general interpretation of Indian culture [5].

Almost every document Las Casas ever prepared concerned the Indians, from the time he began to present

---

[1] Antonio de Remesal gives a number of royal instructions on the subject in *Historia general de las Indias occidentales, y particular de la gobernación de Chiapas y Guatemala* (Madrid, 1619), Libro 2, cap. 7.

[2] A convincing illustration of the contribution of the friars in the field of linguistícs alone may be seen in the *Bibliografía española de lenguas indígenas de América* (Madrid, 1892) by Cipriano Muñoz y Manzano (the Conde de Viñaza).

[3] *Historia general de las cosas de Nueva España* (México, 1938), 5 vols., ed. by Wigberto Jiménez Moreno. His method of checking his material by a wise use of informants was especially notable.

[4] The best and most recent edition, with extensive and valuable notes, has been prepared by Alfred M. Tozzer, whose *Landa's Relación de las cosas de Yucatan* was published as volume 18 of the Papers of the Peabody Museum of American Archaeology and Ethnology, Harvard University (Cambridge, 1941).

[5] Use has been made, however, of Las Casas' writings by such modern authorities as Cayetano Coll y Toste, *Prehistoria de Puerto Rico* (San Juan, 1907); J. W. Fewkes, *The aborigines of Porto Rico and neighboring islands* (Washington, 1907); Herbert W. Krieger, *Archeological and historical investigations in Samaná, Dominican Republic* (Washington, 1929), and "The aborigines of the ancient island of Hispaniola" in the *Annual report of the Smithsonian Institution* (Washington, 1929), 473–506, and *Aboriginal Indian pottery of the Dominican republic* (Washington, 1931); Pablo Morales Cabrera, *Puerto Rico indigena* (San Juan, 1932?); Marshall H. Saville, *Turquois mosaic art in ancient Mexico* (New York, 1922); Samuel K. Lathrop, *Pottery of Costa Rica and Nicaragua* (New York, 1926); H. E. D. Pollock, *Round structures of aboriginal Middle America* (Washington, 1936). Some of these writers used the *Apologética Historia* and others the *Historia de las Indias*. James Williams used both in his attack on Leo Wiener's *Africa and the discovery of America* (3 vols., Philadelphia. 1920–22) and he criticized particularly Wiener's failure to use Las Casas in "Christopher Columbus and aboriginal Indian words," *Proceedings of the Twenty-third International Congress of Americanists* (New York, 1930), 816–850.

petitions to the crown in 1516 until his last days half a century later, during which he composed two huge treatises on the conquest of Peru and even induced the Council of the Indies to listen to a formal reading of these indictments of the Spaniards' treatment of the Incas and their vassals. All of the vast bulk of Las Casas' writings is useful for a study of his work as an anthropologist but his principal contributions are to be found in the *History of the Indies,* described in the last chapter, and his *Summary and Apologetic History of the Qualities, Disposition, Description, Soil and Climate of those Lands and the Natural Conditions, Ways of Life, Government and Customs of the People of the Western and Southern Indies which are under the Dominion of the Kings of Castile* [1].

The *Apologetic History* is as detailed and as long as its title promises and when finally published in 1909 required almost seven hundred double-columned printed pages, without an index to guide the reader through its mazes, which may help to explain why the volume is not widely read or consulted today. Its existence was known to William H. Prescott and other historians [2] but, as the

[1] *Apologética historia sumaria cuanto á las cualidades, dispusicion, descripcion, cielo, y suelo destas tierras, y condiciones naturales, policias, repúblicas, maneras de vivir e costumbres de las gentes destas Indias occidentales y meridionales, cuyo imperio soberano pertenece á los Reyes de Castilla* is the full title but on the title page of the printed volume it is *Apologética historia de las Indias,* de Fr. Bartolomé de las Casas (Madrid, 1909). Ed. by Manuel Serrano y Sanz (Nueva biblioteca de autores españoles, tomo 13). Cited as *Apologética historia.*

[2] Roger Wolcott, ed., *Correspondence of William Hickling Prescott* (Boston, 1925), 385. Ernesto de la Torre Villar has demonstrated that Baltasar Dorantes de Carranza used the *Apologética Historia* in his *Sumaria relación de las cosas de la Nueva España* completed in 1604, *Estudios de la historiografía de la Nueva España* (México, 1945), 236–241. The Augustinian Jerónimo Román y Zamora must have had access to a copy of the manuscript for he copied almost verbatim certain chapters for his *Repúblicas de Indias* according to Francisco Ximénez [cited by Adrián Recinos *Popol Vuh* (México, 1947), 43]. Charles Etienne Brasseur de Bourbourg quoted the *Apologetic History* rather fully in *Popol Vuh* (Paris, 1861), and Lord Kingsborough printed chapter 211 in Volume 8 of *Mexican Antiquities,* and fiftyone scattered chapters appeared as an appendix in volume five of the first printed edition of Las Casas' *Historia de las Indias* (Madrid, 1875–76), 397–602. A transcript, made probably in the second quarter of the nineteenth century, is in the Division of Manuscripts of the Library of Congress in Washington, D. C.

editor of the *Apologetic History* stated, "it has remained a book sealed with seven seals, which no one had the curiosity to break or the patience to read" [1].

Las Casas began to bring together this great accumulation of information on Indian life in 1527 while a resident in the Dominican monastery on a hill above Puerto de Plata in Hispaniola during that period of deep dejection which followed the failure of his colonization project in Venezuela [2]. The description of the new land and its inhabitants had been intended originally to form a part of his general *History of the Indies* but he found that the story became so large and diffuse that it would be well to devote a separate volume to it [3]. Apparently he continued to work on the *Apologetic History* over a period of years and had substantially completed it in 1550 when he used the manuscript as his principal weapon in the dispute with Sepúlveda, to be described later [4]. The manuscript eventually turned up in the library of the Academy of History in Madrid and was finally published. Even now, however, the work as a whole has not been subjected to critical scrutiny and evaluation by a trained anthropologist.

As preparation for the writing of such a work, Las Casas had the experience of half a century in America and in Spain dealing with Indian affairs. He had travelled extensively in the islands of the Caribbean, Mexico, and Central America but had never been to Peru, although he had once started to go there [5]. He had known many

---

[1] Manuel Serrano y Sanz, "Doctrinas psicológicas de Fr. Bartolomé de Las Casas", *Revista de archivos, bibliotecas, y museos*, tomo 17 (Madrid, 1907), 59–60.

[2] *Apologética historia*, pp. 8, 81. Other information on the time at which various chapters were written appears on pp. 16, 17, 94, 322, 614.

[3] *Historia de las Indias*, Libro 1, cap. 67.

[4] He says specifically that "ya está escrita la mayor parte", *ibid.*, end of cap. 67. It seems clear from the references Las Casas made to the *Apologética historia* in his *Historia de las Indias* that he completed the former work first. See *Historia de las Indias*, Libro 2, caps. 9 and 26.

[5] *Apologética historia*, p. 88.

of the principal investigators of Indian life from the time of the first, Friar Ramón Pane [1]; he had enjoyed the confidence of many ecclesiastics and of some royal officials who administered New World affairs, and had received hundreds if not thousands of letters and documents on Indian life from widely scattered parts of the Spanish empire. These communications were so numerous that they constituted a formidable archive at his death, and in his will he directed that some of the younger monks in San Gregorio monastery be set to putting them in order so that, as has been mentioned before, "if God decided some day to destroy Spain because of her evil deeds in the New World, evidence of the reasons therefore would not be lacking" [2]. He was also thoroughly familiar with, and cited in his text, the various histories and other descriptive accounts of America that had appeared in print during the preparation of his work [3].

Las Casas lacked, however any real knowledge of Indian languages and had never lived long enough in any one place to become an expert on the Indians of that region, as certain of his principal enemies took pleasure in pointing out [4]. Of course many distinguished missionaries in the early years of the conquest did not learn Indian languages because of their many other preoccupations; [5] the difficulty of the languages themselves

---

[1] *Ibid.*, pp. 321–23, 345. Chap. 166 (pp. 444–445) is based on an account by Friar Ramón.

[2] Antonio María Fabié, *Vida y escritos de don fray Bartolomé de Las Casas.* I (Madrid, 1879), 237. Many letters and documents directed to Las Casas on Indian affairs may be found in *Documentos inéditos de América*, tomo 7 and in tomo 2 of Fabié, *op. cit.*

[3] Some of the printed material cited: Pedro Martyr, *Opus epistolarum*; *La relación y comentarios del gobernador Alvar Núñez Cabeza de Vaca de lo acaescido en las dos jornadas que hizo a las Indias*; Fernando Cortés, *Cartas*; Miguel de Estete, *Relación de la conquista del Perú.*

[4] Toribio de Benavente (Motolinía) in his famous letter to Charles V against Las Casas, Lesley B. Simpson, *The Encomienda in New Spain* (Berkeley, 1929), 258.

[5] Robert Ricard cites Martín de Valencia, Jacobo de Testera, and Domingo de Betanzos, *La Conquête spirituelle du Mexique* (Paris, 1933), 70–71.

always constituted a serious obstacle [1]. Las Casas kept in touch with many ecclesiastics who had been able to learn the language. One such was the Dominican Domingo de Santo Tomás, who announced in the prologue to his study of Indian languages in Peru that his principal intention of offering to the king his account of the beauty and intricacies of the Indian languages was that "Your Majesty might see very clearly how false is the idea — as many would persuade Your Majesty — that the natives of Peru are barbarians" [2]. And as Professor of Theology in the University of St. Mark in Lima, Santo Tomás undertook to defend the rationality of the Indians against all comers [3].

Las Casas recognized that a command of Indian languages was essential to a true understanding of their culture, particularly their military organization and history, and always took pains to give the accentuation of Indian words used in his text [4] and warned against the erroneous accounts of those who had only a "bread and butter" knowledge of the languages and slight experience in America [5]. He proudly and pointedly informed his readers:

> To avoid such errors, all that I write down concerning Indians in the islands or in the many provinces of Terra Firme is based upon my own experience of over forty years in the New World — and no one living has had as much experience — or upon the knowledge of ecclesiastics who knew the Indians and their language well, with whom I usually travelled; or upon information which I sought by correspondence from the most informed

[1] Francisco Antonio de Fuentes y Guzmán, *Recordación florida,* III (Guatemala, 1933), 408–410.

[2] Cipriano Muñoz y Manzano (conde de Viñaza), *Bibliografía española de lenguas indígenas de América* (Madrid, 1892), 15–16.

[3] Felipe Barreda y Laos, *La vida intelectual de la colonia* (Lima, 1909), 106.

[4] *Apologética historia,* p. 113, gives a typical example of this.

[5] *Ibid.,* p. 175.

ecclesiastics. And much of this work comes from such letters, or from the accounts of other persons whose descriptions seem to me to be reliable [1].

The *Apologetic History* was not, however, a scientific treatise, but a work designed to prove that the Indians were rational beings with such "excellent, most subtle and natural intelligence" that they satisfied all of the requirements laid down by Aristotle for the good life! [2].

Now how did it happen that Las Casas, who years earlier had referred to Aristotle as a "gentile burning in hell whose doctrine should be accepted only so far as it conformed to Christian thought" [3], had found it necessary to write a tremendous volume in which Aristotle was held up as a great authority? To understand this apparent contradiction we must recall the sermons of Antonio de Montesinos and the bitter disputes concerning the true nature of the New World natives, referred to in the first lecture, and to the grievous defeat Las Casas had suffered when Charles V revoked the most stringent provisions of the *New Laws* in 1545 [4]. Friar Antonio de Montesinos had demanded in 1511 that the colonists of Hispaniola tell by what justice they profited from Indian labor and waged war against the defenseless natives, and the questions had never been answered to the satisfaction of the reform group. Las Casas and his supporters had failed to have the encomienda system suppressed, so that the next logical step from their viewpoint was to work for the suppression of all further

[1] *Ibid.*, p. 176.

[2] *Ibid.*, pp. 98–127.

[3] *Obras escojidas de filósofos,* in: Biblioteca de autores españoles, LXV, 227. The frequency with which Las Casas cited the works of Aristotle may be seen in Carlos Larrazabal Blanco, "Bibliografía colonial. Fray Bartolomé de Las Casas," *Clio,* IX (Ciudad Trujillo, 1941), 63–64.

[4] The following paragraphs are based upon a previous study by the writer, *La lucha por justicia en la conquista de América* (Buenos Aires, 1949), Tercera parte, cap. 4.

wars and conquests, so that the evil of Indian slavery could grow no larger.

In this endeavor the greatest obstacle Las Casas encountered was the public proclamation by a famous classical scholar of the time, Juan Ginés de Sepúlveda, that the wars were just largely on account of the rude nature of the Indians, and his strong advocacy of the Aristotelian doctrine that certain human beings were slaves by nature which was invoked to support the Spanish claim that the Indians should serve their conquerors. A great debate was held in 1550 and 1551 at Valladolid before a special council of eminent theologgians, administrators and jurists, who, after hearing both Las Casas and Sepúlveda, apparently were too stupefied by the sheer weight of the many authorities cited by the antagonists to render a formal judgment, or at least never did so. The details of this interesting scholastic combat cannot be given here [1], but for our purpose now it is sufficient to point out that the authority of Aristotle in Spain about 1550 was strong enough to lead Las Casas to draw up his *Apologetic History* within the Aristotelian framework in order to meet and defeat Sepúlveda on the ground this scholar had himself chosen [2].

An analysis of this magisterial *Apologetic History* reveals that in every one of the two hundred and sixty-seven chapters Las Casas was remembering that in describing the Indians he was proving that they did not fit into Aristotle's classification of slaves by nature and that further Indian enslavement in America was thus unjust and unpermissible.

In the first thirty-two chapters of the treatise Las

---

[1] A detailed account may be found in the author's "La controversia entre Las Casas y Sepúlveda en Valladolid, 1550–1551," *Universidad católica bolivariana*, VIII (Medellín, Colombia, 1942), 65–97.)

[2] The argument Las Casas presented has not yet been printed but remains in manuscript in the Bibliothèque Nationale (Paris), Nouveau fonds latin, ms. no. 12926.

Casas describes minutely the favorable physical conditions in the New World which make it inevitable that the Indians are men of wise understanding [1]. Here he shows himself a forerunner of Jean Bodin, usually considered the first European environmentalist. A province by province record of the plants and animals to be found in Hispaniola occupies the first chapter, and there is much data on how the Indians made cassaba bread [2], on their way of generating fire by twirling sticks [3], on herbs used by the natives, and on the question of the origin of syphilis [4]. In the chapter on "The Ill Effects of Sadness and Fear" [5] he comes to conclusions which a modern biologist, the late Walter B. Cannon, demonstrated scientifically in his *Bodily Changes in Fear, Pain, Hunger, and Rage* [6].

All of this detail serves to support the main point of these early chapters: that the physical conditions of the New World (whether one considers the position of the stars, the mild climate or the excellent food grown) have favored the development of human beings with good judgment, understanding, capacity, and physical beauty. It follows necessarily that the Indians are temperate beings with good judgment and understanding, though Las Casas does not assert that all Indians are perfect [7], nor claim that all of the New World enjoys an

---

[1] *Apologética historia,* pp. 1–82.

[2] *Ibid.,* pp. 29–32.

[3] *Ibid.,* pp. 34–35.

[4] Las Casas was interested in finding out whether syphilis had existed in America, enquired into the subject particularly by questioning the Indians and concluded that the disease was to be found in the New World before Columbus arrived. *Ibid.,* p. 44. The best modern discussions of this complicated subject, are by Samuel E. Morison, *Admiral of the Ocean Sea,* II (Boston, 1942), 193–218, and George C. Shattuck, "Syphilis in Yucatan," in *The peninsula of Yucatan* (Washington, 1932), 249–289.

[5] *Apologética historia,* pp. 67–69. See also pp. 55–56 and 70–76.

[6] Walter B. Cannon, *Bodily changes in pain, hunger, fear and rage* (New York, 1915.)

[7] *Apologética historia,* p. 89. "No queremos aquí decir ni afirmar que todos, universalmente, en todos sus actos actualmente sean perfectos y muy acendrados

ideal climate. Hot regions like Panama and Vera Cruz he considers, however, to be exceptional [1].

It follows, too, that the Indians are of an extraordinary beauty, and Las Casas mentions the provinces where the most perfectly formed men and women live [2]. This explains, he feels, the eagerness of Spaniards to take Indian women as wives. The Indians' sobriety in food and drink is another notable characteristic whose value is emphasized by quotations from Paul, Peter, Plato, and Aristotle [3]. This sobriety makes for large families of attractive children, and Las Casas cites the case of an Indian woman in Mexico City who in one day gave birth to five children — the first record of an American predecessor to the Dionne quintuplets! [4].

Though the islands have no great buildings, imposing town walls or magnificent cities, the natives live together in friendship and peace, united by strong voluntary bonds and thus fulfill the most important requirement for a good and permanent state [5]. Las Casas points out that only an extraordinarily peaceful people could crowd in such numbers into straw houses and live under one roof without discord [6]. Any ex-serviceman who has brought his wife and children to live with relatives until the housing situation improves can testify to the sweetness of temper and strength of character required under such conditons!

Never is any particular attention paid to the defects

---

en las obras de perfecta razón, sino que todos universalmente y por la mayor parte tienen natural aptitud y habilidad, y muy de propincuo están en potencia para ser reducidos al acto y actos, siendo instruídos, de todo buen entendimiento y de buena razón, y finalmente, que son hombres de su naturaleza bien razonables y bien inclinados, y dello tienen muy ciertos y naturales indicios y claras señales."

[1] *Ibid.*, p. 52.

[2] *Ibid.*, pp. 83–89.

[3] *Ibid.*, pp. 89–91.

[4] *Ibid.*, p. 91.

[5] *Ibid.*, pp. 119, 122.

[6] *Ibid.*, pp. 120–121.

and bad customs of the Indians, for Las Casas frankly confesses that his attitude is not to emphasize such things but rather to marvel at the favorable aspects of the lives of these pagans who have lived without God and the blessings of Christianity [1]. He made this viewpoint clear in chapter 48, the most important one in the whole volume doctrinally, which is entitled "How All Nations May Be Brought To A Good Way of Life."

All peoples started out in a rude state and even the Greeks had to be taught to live together under a common law and to keep only one woman as a wife. After citing examples ranging from the time of King Rhadamantus of Lycia to King Zechio of Bulgaria, Las Casas roundly declares:

> Thus we clearly see, by examples ancient and modern, that no nation exists, no matter how rude, uncultivated, barbarous, gross, or almost brutal its people may be, which may not be persuaded and brought to a good order and way of life, and made domestic, mild, and tractable, provided the method that is proper and natural to men is used; namely, love, gentleness and kindness [2].

Las Casas would have enthusiastically supported the statement of the eighteenth-century Jesuit historian Francisco Javier Clavigero, who declared: "Never did Europeans more wrongly employ their reasoning faculties than when they doubted the rationality of the American Indians" [3]. Even the wandering savages of the coast of Florida are rational men who may be taught. They are merely in that rude state which all other nations existed in before receiving instruction.

Las Casas now sets up a record set of norms — this time in an effort to ascertain what is necessary if a republic

---

[1] *Ibid.*, p. 118.
[2] *Ibid.*, pp. 127–128.
[3] *Estudios de la historiografía de la Nueva España* (México, 1945), p. 317.

is to be permanent and self-sufficient. Again he follows Aristotle to the letter; the six essentials are taken over wholesale from the *Politics.* They are: (1) workers to cultivate the soil; (2) artificers who perform necessary work for the community; (3) warriors to defend the city from aggression and to constrain those who do not want to obey the laws; (4) men of wealth; (5) priests to offer sacrifices; (6) judges.

Then follows a wondrous procession of two hundred and thirty six chapters loaded down with meticulous detail. Las Casas ranges from Thebes to Cuzco, from Homer to Thomas Aquinas. One venerable authority after another is invoked to lend theoretical significance to this avalanche of facts, which overwhelms the reader not previously inured to the discursiveness of Las Casas. As illustration of the encyclopedic tendency of his mind, he finds it necessary in the course of the argument in these two hundred and sixty-six chapters to write whole chapters on the vestal virgins, volcanoes in Nicaragua, the origin of idolatry, demonology, Greek temples, magic, Chaldean gods, fiestas in Honduras, as well as a chapter which establishes the comforting fact that the fire of volcanoes is not the fire of hell! Such chapter headings as "How Men May Be Transformed by Magic into Beasts," "How the Devil Tries to Get Us and Remedies Against Him," "The Opinions of the Indians on the Way the Earth Was Populated after the Flood," show what a variegated feast is spread before the reader. Nor is Las Casas intimidated by the authority of the ancient world, for he maintains that the Maya temples in Yucatan are not less worthy of admiration than the Pyramids, thus anticipating the judgment of twentieth-century archaeologists.

Throughout this welter of fact and fantasy, Las Casas not only strives to show that Indian society provides the six conditions enumerated above, but he also develops the idea that the Greeks and Romans were, in several respects, inferior to the American Indians. The Indians are clearly more religious, for instance, because they offer more and better sacrifices to their gods than did any of the ancient peoples. The Mexican Indians are superior to the ancient peoples in rearing and educating their children. Their marriage arrangements are reasonable and conform to natural law and the law of nations. Indian women are devout workers, even laboring with their hands if necessary to comply fully with divine law, a trait which many Christian matrons might well copy. At this point Las Casas exhibits somewhat the same spirit that animated Clement of Alexandria, who extolled barbarian inventions at the expense of Athens, and the moralist Tacitus, who constantly held up the virtues of the barbarian Germans as examples to the degenerate citizens of Rome. Las Casas concludes from this stupifying array of evidence that the Indians are no less rational than the Egyptians, Romans, or Greeks and are not much inferior to Spaniards. Indeed, in some respects they are even superior to Spaniards [1].

It is not so clear to us today, and of course it all depends on which class of Indians you are contrasting with which class of Spaniards. Alexander von Humboldt was to write, centuries after the Valladolid dispute:

> There are countries in northern Europe where, not withstanding the boasted civilization of the higher classes of society, the peasant still lives in the same degradation under which he groaned three or four centuries ago. We should think higher, perhaps, of the situation of the Indians were we to compare it with that of the peasants of Courland, Russia, and a great part of the north of Germany [2].

Apparently no one was sophisticated or honest enough

[1] *Apologética historia*, p. 138.

[2] Alexander von Humboldt, *Political essay on the kingdom of New Spain*, I (London, 1811), 134.

LIBRARY OF MOUNT ST. MARY'S COLLEGE EMMITSBURG, MARYLAND

in Spain to arise, as did Montaigne in France, to declare that everyone terms "barbaric" that which is not according to his own custom, though Las Casas pointed out that it is just as barbarous for Spaniards not to speak Indian languages as for Indians not to speak Spanish!

The slight defects Las Casas discovers in Indian character are of no great significance to him and do not deflect the onward march of the irresistible argument. Although he admits that marriage arrangements on Hispaniola are rather lax, he devotes the following three chapters to explaining how much worse conditions obtained in ancient times.

In the course of this purposeful meandering, Las Casas turns to his final set of standards for the good life which follows closely the list as given in Aristotle's *Politics.* The three conditions essential for the good life are: (1) that the group be joined together in a unity of peace; (2) that this group be guided in order to attain the good life; (3) that the industry of the group be sufficient for its needs. The last thirty or forty chapters of the *Apologetic History* show that the Indians also meet these three requirements.

The anthropologist patient enough to mine in these chapters will find many useful nuggets of information hidden away, mostly in the descriptions of the Indians' skills and accomplishments. Their agricultural methods are particularized as well as their irrigation systems;[1] their ingenuity is illustrated by the way they derive twenty-two products from the maguey tree,[2] contrive delicate ornamental collars of fish bones, and create

[1] *Apologética historia,* pp. 151–155. Much miscellaneous and curious information is given by Las Casas-such as the fact that he could read his prayers by the illumination provided by lightning bugs (p.7), that the smell of the male crocodile was so penetrating that he could remember it for sixteen years (p. 27), and that he had heard birds sing in three voices (p. 9). He also states that some of the Indian women of the islands were so expert with the bow that they could shoot accurately while swimming in rivers and in the sea (p. 171).

[2] *Ibid.*, p. 153.

remarkable gold jewelry, [1] a fact which may be confirmed today by a visit to any well-stocked museum or by reference to such a volume as Lathrop's on the Coclé Indians [2]. Special attention is drawn to the extraordinary capacity the Indians displayed in learning the Old World crafts which the Spaniards had brought with them [3], an enthusiactic recital which Las Casas brings to an end with a careful account, evidently based on prolonged personal observation, of the way the Indians made knives [4]. Las Casas also describes how the Indians made rubber balls, the cleverness of their painters, their feather work, silver making with few tools, and, after little training, their competence in fashioning musical instruments, [5] their work as carpenters, and their hand lettering which is so fine that it sometimes cannot be distinguished from printing [6]. The only thing he finds the Indian cannot do as well as Spaniards is to shoe horses. Their mining methods are described and this long paean of praise for Indian skill also includes an account of an Indian ball game [7]. Above all, however, the Indians excel in the dramatic arts and various illustrations are given to demonstrate this [8].

---

[1] *Ibid.*, p. 156–157.

[2] Samuel K. Lothrop, *Coché, an archaeological study* (Cambridge, 1937).

[3] *Ibid.*, p. 158.

[4] *Ibid.*, p. 159.

[5] *Ibid.*, p. 161. Jerónimo de Mendieta greatly praised Indian music ability saying "una cosa puedo afirmar con verdad, que en todos los reinos de cristianidad (fuera de las Indias) no hay tanta copia de flautas, chirimías, sacabuches, orlos, trompetas, y atabales, como en solo este reino de la Nueva España". *Historia eclesiástica indiana* (México, 1870), Lib. 4, cap. 14, pp. 412–413. Ed. by Joaquín García Icazbalceta. There were also complaints that Indians became too much interested in music, spent too much money on instruments, and in general required more supervision in its practice if excess were not to result. Archivo de Indias (Sevilla), México 291. These statements appear in a memorial on various ecclesiastical questions by the three provincials in New Spain to the Council of the Indies.

[6] *Apologética historia,* p. 162.

[7] *Ibid.*, pp. 167–170.

[8] *Ibid.*, pp. 162–165.

The military organization of both the Mexican Indians and the Incas of Peru [1], a topic on which relatively little data is provided by other works, is described by Las Casas and much information is given on their coca chewing, and tobacco smoking, and an excellent description of the great teeming market in Mexico City [2].

Many pages are devoted to the religion of the Indians, and the most striking aspect of this section is the attitude Las Casas adopted toward Indian sacrifices [3]. He considered that the most religious nations were those which offered to God the most magnificent sacrifice, and those who offered human beings had — in his opinion — a very noble concept indeed of their God [4]. The Indian fasts, mortifications of the body, sacrifices of animals and men, were clearly superior to the sacrifices of the ancient peoples. Under the horrible and bloody aspects of these rites, Las Casas discerned a commendable spirit of devotion which could be directed to higher ends and enlisted in the service of the only true God [5].

The following conclusion to his description of the Inca worship of the sun, as established by the ruler Pacachuti Inga, reveals in him the sympathetic understanding and tolerance which is the mark of every good anthropologist:

> It is worthy of note and much consideration that King Pacachuti, without a knowledge of the true God, could, with only the light of natural reason to guide him, come to know that many of the gods previously worshipped by the Peruvians were not worthy of veneration and instead he at least chose, even though he erred in so doing, the most excellent work of God and thus recognized and confessed faintly that one should render honor and reverence to the best one knows.

---

[1] *Ibid.*, pp. 173–178.

[2] *Ibid.*, pp. 181–182.

[3] *Ibid.*, pp. 483–509.

[4] *Ibid.*, p. 481.

[5] *Ibid.*, p. 494–506.

Let us also ponder the fact that if such a king should accept the faith and know the true God, what great temples, ministers, ceremonies and sacrifices would he not establish for the honor of God and the exercise of the Christian religion? Even though he could not improve on his present achievements, he would be able to conduct the religious devotions with greater certainty and confidence of a response, and with a softer and more intimate attitude than he can display toward the sun.

With this we close our account of the gods worshipped in more than three thousand leagues of the lands of our Indies, and we may thus conclude that all the rest of the nations, even though we have no notice of them, are, more or less, similar to those we already know in matters of religion [1].

The disgusting customs Las Casas mentions from time to time he explains away or shows that Spaniards have had quite as revolting habits. Even the Indians' habit of eating their own head lice, which they defended by saying it was really their own flesh and blood, Las Casas is able to show as less offensive than at least one Tartar custom [2]. Las Casas denounces flesh eating by Indians but does not consider that this habit alone proves that they cannot govern themselves and suspects that they learned it of the Scythians [3].

The laws of the Mexican Indians are given in great detail — this perhaps to impress such a juridical people as the Spaniards — all statements being carefully collected and authenticated by ecclesiastics who know the language and have special knowledige of such matters. The signed and duly authorized manuscripts are, says Las Casas, in his possession as he writes [4].

---

[1] *Ibid.*, p. 336.
[2] *Ibid.*, p. 537.
[3] *Ibid.*, pp. 539–540.
[4] *Ibid.*, pp. 559–575.

Furthermore, the Mexican Indians pay meticulous attention to the education of their children in the ways of chastity, honesty, fortitude, obedience, and sobriety. Indeed, some Christians might well learn in these matters from the Indians! The exhortations given by fathers (even humble laborers) to their sons, and by mothers to their daughters have particularly impressed Las Casas, who cries:

> Did Plato, Socrates, Pythagoras, or even Aristotle leave us better or more natural or more necessary exhortations to the virtuous life than these barbarians delivered to their children? Does the Christian religion teach us more, save the faith and what it teaches us of invisible and supernatural matters? Therefore, no one may deny that these people are fully capable of governing themselves and of living like men of good intelligence and more than others well ordered, sensible, prudent, and rational [1].

Las Casas, looking back on the New World in which he has lived so long, sees a vast region of smiling valleys, well cultivated by an intelligent people who have created monuments, laws, and a way of life worthy of admiration. At times he is so lyrical that he checks himself to assure the reader solemnly that all these things are true; [2] that he has either seen them with his own eyes or has faithfully transcribed what some reputable person has written, for "God has no need for me to compose falsehoods, and thus exceed the bounds of truth, since they manifestly offend Him, and I do not set them down here, nor repeat them or suffer them" [3]. Las Casas' summing up, in the closing chapters of this extraordinary work, stresses his conclusion that the American Indians are simply mild, as yet unchristianized barbarians who can, on no account, be considered in the category of

---

[1] *Ibid.*, p. 589.
[2] *Ibid.*, p. 138.
[3] *Ibid.*, p. 575.

JUAN GINES DE SEPÚLVEDA
Cordobes: Theólogo, crítico, filólogo, é Histo
riador: nació en 1490. y murió
en 1573.

barbarians who are slaves by nature according to the Aristotelian dictum [1].

As one studies the use made by both contestants of Aristotle's theory of slavery, the doubt arises whether either Las Casas or Sepúlveda had as firm a grasp on the theory as each was absolutely certain he had. Even today the theory has its obscurities and, as a modern interpreter declares, "it must be confessed that Aristotle in no place clearly indicates how a true slave may be known from a free man" [2]. In the absence of any clear definition of a slave, both contestants were free to interpret Aristotle according to their own lights. One wonders how the welter of information set forth by the antagonists to support their irreconcilable views impressed the judges as they sat through the length sessions in those hot August days in Valladolid in 1550, and the subsequent meetings in the following year. The judges must have been both bewildered and fatigued. We know that they never reached a collective decision.

Perhaps it is appropriate here to point out that the Valladolid disputation has often been over simplified as a clearcut dispute between a Christian apostle and a Renaissance humanist of Aristotelian persuasion. On the other hand, one contemporary Mexican writer, Edmundo O'Gorman, finds a paradox in the Valladolid confrontation of the two antagonists and has announced that to his mind all of Las Casas' thought is fundamentally Aristotelian, while Sepúlveda is not less a Christian than Las Casas [3].

It is true that Las Casas in his argument appears to accept the theory of Aristotle that some men are by

[1] *Ibid.*, pp. 683–695.

[2] Robert O. Schlaifer, "Greek theories of slavery from Homer to Aristotle," *Harvard studies in classical philology*, no. 47 (Cambridge, 1936), pp. 165–204. See also E. E. Sikes, *Anthropology of the Greeks* (London, 1914), 73.

[3] Edmundo O'Gorman, "Sobre la naturaleza bestial del indio americano," *Filosofía y letras*, no. 2 (México, 1941), p. 312.

nature slaves. But the important point here is his vigorous assertion that the Indians of the New World, as peoples, do not fall into this category. Las Casas does not contest the Aristotelian theory of natural slavery but believes that these slaves are few in number, and must be considered as mistakes of nature, like men born with six toes or only one eye. Such cases occur very infrequently, for the Creator would never have brought into being such monstrosities, "against the natural inclination of all the peoples of the world". From this basic concept Las Casas draws the following conclusion which is certainly Christian rather than Aristotelian and which has no counterpart in Sepúlveda's argument:

> All the nations of the world are men .... all have understanding and volition, all have the five exterior senses and the four interior senses, and are moved by the objects of these, all take satisfaction in goodness and feel pleasure with happy and delicious things, all regret and abhor evil [1].

Las Casas has faith in the capacity for civilization of all peoples; he does not believe in a static and hopeless barbarism, but in social mobility. Las Casas would certainly have objected to the idea of the eighteenth-century Jesuits who, in reply to critics inquiring why no attempt was made to elevate Indians into free agents, replied that they were only full grown children (*bambini con barba*), [2] for Las Casas insisted:

> No nation exists today, nor could exist, no matter how barbarous, fierce, or depraved its custom may be, which may not be attracted and converted to all political virtues, and to all the humanity of domestic political, and rational man [3].

To bring this about Las Casas would not enslave the

---

[1] Las Casas, *Historia de las Indias,* Lib. 2. cap. 58.

[2] Robert Southey, *History of Brazil* (London, 1817), p. 363.

[3] *Apologética historia,* p. 128.

Indians but would treat them as free human beings who would doubtless accept the faith if only it were preached to them peacefully and not by warlike methods — an idea very dear to him which he had set forth in his treatise of 1537 entitled *The Only Method To Attract All People to the True Religion* [1].

It is true that Las Casas did not at Valladolid attempt to defend the character of all peoples in the world, nor did he work there for any liberty except Indian liberty, but throughout his writings he fought the idea that slavery was good for the men he saw in the New World, whether Indians or Negroes. He had once, early in his career, advised that Negroes born as slaves in Spain should be brought to work in America, to spare the Indians, but soon after declared that, since he had learned that the Negroes had been captured and enslaved unjustly, he now believed "that it is as unjust to enslave Negroes as Indians, and for the same reasons." [2] But he was so intent on saving the Indians that his arguments at Valladolid and elsewhere rarely rose to the level of general theories but were usually contentions relating to justice for the Indians.

Sepúlveda, on the other hand, emphasized the fact that the tutelage of the inferior Indians by the superior Spaniards would result in their Christianization eventually. Here he was applying, in a Christian world, the Aristotelian doctrine that the superior governors should rule in the interest of the Indians. Otherwise the Spanish

---

[1] Printed in Mexico in 1941 as *Del único modo de atraer a todos los pueblos a la verdadera religión*. An analysis and critique of it are given by Edmundo O'Gorman in his *Fundamentos de la historia de América* (México, 1942). For the writer's dissent from O'Gorman's interpretation, see *The Spanish Struggle for Justice in the Conquest of America*, pp. 187-189.

[2] See Silvio Zavala, "Las Casas, esclavista?" *Cuadernos americanos*, año 3 (México, 1944), no. 2. pp. 149-154. José Antonio Saco made the definitive defense of Las Casas against charges that he supported Negro slavery in his *Historia de la esclavitud de la raza africana en el mundo nuevo y en especial en los paises américo-hispanos*, I (Barcelona, 1879), 100–109.

rule would be tyrannical. Thus Sepúlveda was neither a suave pagan supporting vicious doctrines, as some nineteenth-century writers charged, nor a sixteenth-century Nietzche, as a more recent writer states. Neither do we need to accept the dictum of a frankly enthusiastic biographer, that Sepúlveda's theory of slavery reveals "the balanced sanity of a great mind." Of course, he was not alone among his contemporaries in his support of Aristotle's doctrine of slavery. In fact, he represents that curious and not wholly amalgamated mixture of Aristotelianism and Christianity that is observable in the thought of many Renaissance figures.

This much, however, is true. At a time when the conquistadores were bringing to the notice of the civilized world a whole new continent peopled with strange races, he chose to regard all these new peoples as an inferior type of humanuty which should be submitted to the rule Spaniards. Without having seen the Indians or observed their lands and civilization, he felt no hesitation in pronouncing them not quite men, above monkeys to be sure, but unworthy of being considered in the same class with the Spaniards.

The solemnity with which Aristotle's doctrine of slavery and its application to the complicated situation of the New World were debated at Valladolid is all the more ironical in view of the diversity of races and cultures in America. Aristotle believed that the state ought to consist of a single race, for a single race is united in its customs and habits which makes for friendship between citizens by reason of their likeness one to another. Spanish America has never had such unity. As the liberator Simón Bolívar pointed out at the Congress of Angostura in 1819:

> It is impossible to say to which human family we belong. The larger part of the native population has disappeared. Europeans have mixed with the Indians and the Negroes, and Negroes have mixed

> with Indians. We were all born of one mother, America, though our fathers had different origins and we all have differently colored skins. This dissimilarity is of the greatest significance [1].

Las Casas never sought to break down the Aristotelian theory as did those earlier philosophers who in the Hellenistic period substituted for the doctrine of slavery by nature the concept of the universal brotherhood of man. Las Casas took the easier way. He accepted but never attempted to defend or extend Aristotle's doctrine although he definitely worked within its framework. By lauding the virtues of all the Indians as though they were a single nation, he laid himself open to grave charges, since the Indian nations were in fact so diverse, being besides on different levels of civilization. As Roberto Levillier has pointedly asked, Which Indians of which regions were these theologians talking about?

> Indians were the Tekestas and Tahinos of Duba, mild and hospitable; Indians, the cannibalistic Caribs; Indians, the primitive Otomi who lived in caves; Indians, the savage Jivaros; Indians, the Uros, more fish than man, who lived in the waters of Lake Titicaca; Indians, the artistic Maya stone cutters and the Chibcha jewelry craftsmen and the wise Inca legislators and the delicate Yunga ceramic workers; and the Colla weavers; Indians, the heroic Aztecs, the cannibalistic Chiriguanaes, and the untamed Diaguitas and Araucanians; Indians, the timid Juri, the nomadic Iule, the sedentary Comechingon, the fierce Guarani. Their intelligence, cruelty, and meekness varied as did the color of their skins, their languages, their rites, their theogonies, and the true owners were confused with those who subjected them to obedience. Neither in their juridical position, in their physical aspect, in their language

---

[1] Simón Bolívar, *Discursos y proclamas* (Paris, 1913), 47. Ed. by Rufino Blanco-Fombona.

> in their tastes, in their morality, nor in their creative capacities were they alike [1].

Neither Las Casas nor Sepúlveda provided an answer to this question which seems to Levillier and the rest of us today so reasonable. Sepúlveda believed that as the Indians became better acquainted with Christianity and European habits, they should be granted greater freedom. But even conversion, he maintained, did not necessarily make an Indian equal to a Spaniard or entitle him to political independence. He could be quoted, therefore, in support of the perpetual encomienda, which was being pressed hotly on the crown at that time by the conquistadores through their representatives in Spain. In effect, Sepúlveda seems to have advocated a permanent mandate for Spain over the peoples of the New World.

Though the judges rendered no formal decision, the struggle Las Casas undertook at Valladolid, with the *Apologetic History* as his principal weapon, had a special significance in the history of America. At a time when many men doubted whether the Indians could be saved at all, Las Casas lifted his voice in their behalf and exerted all "his godly zeal of converting soules to Jesus Christ from the power of Ethnicke darkness", as the Elizabethans described it, and exclaimed, as did Montesinos forty years before on the island of Hispaniola: "Are these Indians not men? Do they not have rational minds? Are you not obliged to love them as you love yourselves?"

When considered in this way, the disputation at Valladolid in 1550 and 1551 stands forth clearly, not as a personal struggle between a friar and a scholar, not merely as a loud argument to approve or disapprove the printing of Sepúlveda's treatise, but as the passionate record of a crucial event in the history of mankind. Be-

---

[1] Roberto Levillier, *Don Francisco de Toledo*, I (Buenos Aires, 1935), 178.

cause Sepúlveda's ideas failed there to win official approval, Spain, through the mouth of Las Casas, made a substantial contribution toward the development of one of the most important hypotheses ever set forth — the idea that the Indians discovered in Spains' onward rush through the lands of the New World were not beasts, not slaves by nature, not childlike creatures with a limited understanding, but men capable of becoming Christians, with the right to enjoy their property, political liberty, and human dignity, who should be incorporated into the Spanish and Christian civilization rather than enslaved or destroyed. One more painful and faltering step was thus taken along the road of justice for all races in a world of many races. For when Las Casas spoke at Valladolid for the American Indians his argumentation had another usefulness: it strengthened the hands of all those who in his time and in the centuries to follow worked in the belief that all the peoples of the world are human beings with the potentialities and responsibilities of men.

Now to return to the original question posed at the beginning of this chapter. Even though Las Casas devoted much attention to Indian culture, may we still call him an anthropologist? In weighing the evidence on this point, it must be admitted that his eagerness to study Indian life rested upon a definite and preconceived idea — the theory that these newly discovered men and women had souls and could learn to govern their own destinies. To offset this, however, he conducted his search for these facts by interviewing and learning from those Spaniards who mastered Indian languages and were in the best position to know the truth. His citation of numerous published and manuscript accounts sets him apart from most of his contemporaries and even from some anthropologists today who disdain or at least who do not use much historical evidence because they place greater reliance on direct observation. Las Casas thus occupies a position somewhere between that of an armchair student and that of a field anthropologist who conscientiously remains in the village he is studying from one harvest to the next before he ventures to assert that he knows much about the Indians' way of life.

Las Casas knew what he wanted to prove, just as did those Spaniards who expected, in the early days of the conquest, to find the New World exactly as the Greeks had imagined the first age of mankind on earth to have been [1]. His eyes, like theirs, were bound to see what they expected and wanted to see. Las Casas exaggerated, as did other Spaniards, lay and ecclesiastical, the flourishing state of the lands and peoples across the seas, for the discovery inflamed the imaginations of many men.

He felt, however, the true anthropologists concern to rescue all possible information on the languages and customs of the vanishing people of the earth, and lamented the fact that he did not record data on certain tribes he had known that were afterwards completely exterminated [2]. Even though Las Casas had an axe to grind and studied Indian cultures only incidentally, in order to influence the course of events in America, his contributions to the field of anthropology were considerable. For his recognition and insistence that the Indians had developed a civilization of their own which was worthy of study and, even more, worthy of respect, sets him apart from his contemporaries and constitutes his principal claim to be considered an anthropologist [3].

Apparently the careful and honest study of other cultures is a recent and not wholly completed achievement of modern scholarship, and the learned and lively controversies which make anthropology one of the most inte-

[1] Alexander von Humboldt, *A personal narrative of travels to the equinoctial regions of America, during the years* 1799–1804, Vol. 2 (London, 1876), 400.

[2] *Apologética historia*, p. 321 and *Historia de las Indias*, Lib. I, cap. 67.

[3] To appreciate how Las Casas differed from other anthropologists, see Franz Boas, "The history of anthropology," *Science*, Vol. 40 (1904), 514.

resting fields today indicate that even now personal attitudes play a considerable role [1]. As Levy-Bruhl states in describing some modern anthropologists, "their eyes seem to be screened in a way which prevents them from perceiving any fact not provided for in their catechism and, in relating what they do see, their preconceived interpretation can no longer be distinguished from the facts themselves". [2]. Almost all anthropologists today, however, are aggressively articulate in explaining that there is no such thing as immutable races, that differences between peoples are to be studied not derided, and that the so-called civilized world can learn to some extent at least from the more primitive peoples of the earth [3].

Las Casas placed all of his enormous vitality and intellectual curiosity at the service of these ideas. For a sixteenth-century Spaniard this was a most remarkable point of view, which reveals Las Casas as a towering figure of his own time, with many attributes of a twentieth-century thinker. Despite the obvious defects and prejudices of Las Casas' work, anthropologists of our own time need be neither surprised nor embarrassed to find him in the company of their distinguished forerunners.

---

[1] An interesting survey of the development in the United States during the last seventy-five years of ethnological theory, with copious bibliographical notes, is given by Leslie A. White, "Evolucionismo e anti-evolucionismo na teoría etnológica americana", *Sociologia,* X (São Paulo, 1948), 1–39. It is instructive to note that anthropologists have long stirred up controversy. Paul Broca met with great obstacles from those in authority when he started to organize the Société d'anthropologie de Paris in 1859. A police officer, in plain clothes, attended each meeting and reported to the prefect the tenor of the proceedings. Robert Fletcher, "Paul Broca and the French school of anthropology," *The Saturday lectures delivered in the lecture room of the U.S. National Museum under the auspices of the anthropological and biological societies of Washington* (Washington, 1882), 113–142.

[2] Lucien Levy-Bruhl, *How natives think* (New York, 1926), 32.

[3] I am thinking here of such anthropologists as Franz Boas, Ruth Benedict, Melville Herskovits, Ralph Linton, and Robert Redfield.

Chapter IV

CONCLUSION

The story and the meaning of Spanish efforts to work out just methods of treating the Indians and Indian problems cannot be summed up or easily and confidently "explained". It was not a simple or easy struggle and there was no decisive victory. Even late in the sixteenth century the Jesuit missionary José de Acosta found not only a diversity of opinion on Indian affairs but also that not a few people doubted whether the Indians could be saved.

The historian who is confronted by the mass of printed and manuscript material available on the struggle, or views the colonial monuments in Spanish America which remain to testify to the imperial grandeur that was Spain, can easily see today that the crown and the nation was attempting to achieve the impossible in the sixteenth century. As Spanish rulers, the kings sought imperial dominion, prestige, and revenue — in short, conquest and the fruits of conquest which involve war. As heads of the church in America they were urgently committed to the great enterprise of winning the Indians to the faith — which requires peace. The pursuit of this double purpose made inevitable both a vacillating royal policy and a mighty conflict of ideas and of men. It was the tragedy of the Indians that the accomplishment of either of the two Spanish purposes necessitated the overthrow of established Indian values and the disruption of the Indian cultures.

The sermons of Friar Antonio de Montesinos constituted the opening scene in this tragedy, and his brother Dominican Bartolomé de Las Casas was the principal actor ,though there were many others in the cast. The struggle did not remain an academic exercise carried on by cloistered philosophers in Spain, with learned footnotes as their most deadly weapons. The battle came to be fought by men of action, ecclesiastics as well as conquistadores, who carried their fundamental disagreements to all the distant corners of the empire. Therefore, the class of arms was not the only struggle during the conquest. The clash of ideas that accompanied the discovery of America and the establishment of Spanish rule there is a story that must be told as an integral part of the conquest, and endows it with a unique character worthy of note. Of course, many nations have had a "habit of acting under an odd mixture of selfish and altruistic motives," as Woodrow Wilson expressed it when describing the history of the United States [1]. No European nation, however, with the possible exception of Portugal, took her Christian duty toward native peoples so seriousy as did Spain. Certainly England did not, for as one New England preacher said, "the Puritan hoped to meet the Pequod Indians in heaven, but wished to keep apart from them on earth, nay, to exterminate them from the land" [2].

The Spaniards, or at least many of them, had an entirely different attitude toward the Indians and the desirability of incorporating them into a Christian and European civilization, as the disputes on their character have shown. Those loud and dogmatic voices quarreling over the Indians have a peculiarly human ring, representing as they do opposed theories of human values as well as philosophical and theological differences.

---

[1] *The public papers of Woodrow Wilson*, I (New York, 1925), 101. Ed. by Ray Stannard Baker and William E. Dodd.

[2] Theodore Parker, *Collected works*, X (London, 1865), 121.

The echoes of this sixteenth-century conflict are heard today in every Spanish speaking land. Mexicans, for example, have refused to permit even a picture of Cortés the conquistador to be hung in a public place, while they long ago erected an imposing monument to Las Casas, the Apostle to the Indians, near the cathedral in Mexico, as well as placing his name in a prominent place in the Ministry of Education building along with Quetzalcóatl, Plato, and Buddha [1]. The concept of race, the idea that any group of people is inferior as a group, against which Las Casas fought at Valladolid in 1550, today is so repugnant to some that the First Inter-American Demographic Congress, held in Mexico in 1943, attempted to suppress the use of the word or the concept. In Cuba, as Fernando Ortiz has pointed out, the feeling is so strong against it that there is no „Day of the Race" celebration on October 12, but a "Fiesta in Commemoration of the Discovery of America" [2]. In Guatemala Rafael Arévalo Martínez recently stirred up an extensive and violent controversy in the newspapers by publishing an article entitled "De Aristóteles a Hitler," in which he strongly supported the declaration of Las Casas against the application of Aristotle's theory of natural slavery to the Indians.

The struggle has also had a profound influence on the writing of the history of Spain in America. No other aspect of Spain's colonial history has evoked so continuously such bitter differences of interpretation. One might almost classify historians in this field — as did William Burghardt Dubois in preparing a bibliography on the Negro — according to their attitude toward Indians and their champions [3]. The friars and others who spoke freely of

---

[1] F.S.C. Northrop. *The meeting of east and west* (New York, 1946), 6.

[2] Fernando Ortiz, *El engaño de las razas* (La Habana, 1945), cap. 12.

[3] William Edward Burghardt DuBois, *Black reconstruction* (New York, 1935), 731–737.

Spanish abuses and clamored vigorously for their own concept of justice for the Indians were looked upon at the time either as noble apostles or as impractical trouble-makers. Later on they were charged with being rebels and fanatics, careless of the truth and their nation's honor, or soft, muddle-headed humanitarians.

This divergence persists today and may be best seen in reactions to Las Casas, whose writings have proved themselves to be more durable than brass. His histories, political treatises, anthropological descriptions, as well as his actions, have become recognized as an integral part of the Spanish conquest and no modern student may be said to have understood this great movement until he has confronted the work of Las Casas and reached some judgment on its value, whether favorable or adverse. One writer, in a prominent Madrid newspaper, declared in 1927 that Las Casas was not really in his right mind, and was answered at once by another Spaniard who declared:

> Far from considering Las Casas crazy, we believe that he was a genuinely Spanish figure, exhibiting all the virtues and defects of our race. We must not accuse him of insanity in order to combat his exaggerations. He was a Spaniard through and through. To maintain otherwise is to perpetuate in a certain sense the black legend [1].

The tendency to regard Las Casas and the reformers as true Spaniards has been growing, particularly in Spanish America. The Cuban José María Chacón y Calvo has advocated the view that the widespread criticism permitted, and even stimulated, by the crown really constitutes one of the glories of Spanish civilization [2]. The pendulum is swinging so far in this direction that the

[1] "La locura de Fray Bartolomé de Las Casas," *Revista hispanoamericana de ciencias, letras y artes*, VI (Madrid, 1927), 284–290.

[2] *Criticismo y colonización* (La Habana, 1935), 17.

twenty-sixth Congress of Americanists. which met in Seville in 1935, approved unanimously, although after acrimonious debate, the proposition put forward by various Spanish-American delegates, that the men who criticized Spain's colonial practices — Montesinos, Las Casas, and Vitoria should be considered "as authentic representatives in the New World of the Spanish conscience" [1]. A striking example of this new attitude was exhibited in 1944 by the Cuban Enrique Gay Calbó on the occasion of the unveiling in Havana of a picture of Las Casas. Gay Calbó declared

> We, the American descendants of Spaniards .... believe that the true Spain is not that of Sepúlveda and Charles V, but that of Las Casas and Vitoria .... It appears appropriate to Cubans that in a public building there should be placed the picture of Friar Bartolomé de Las Casas, a true and exemplary Spaniard [2].

This new spirit has not swept all before it, however, for in Mexico one prominent jurist has publicly labelled Las Casas as being very closely related to the Communists, a sort of pre-Marxian who preached the class struggle [3]. In present day Spain, too, publications supporting Sepúlveda have appeared and one of Spain's greatest living scholars, Ramón Menéndez Pidal, recently attacked Las Casas [4].

But in judging these attitudes we must not struggle out of one pit of prejudices to fall into another. Not Las Casas, not Sepúlveda, nor any other single individual

---

[1] Chacón y Calvo, *Cartas censorias de la conquista* (La Habana, 1938), 3–4.

[2] Enrique Gay Calbó, "Discurso sobre Fray Bartolomé de Las Casas," *Boletln del archivo nacional*, XLI (La Habana, 1942), 106.

[3] Toribio Esquivel Obregón, *Apuntes para la historia del derecho en México*, II (México, 1937), 61.

[4] Menéndez Pidal delivered his attack in an article "Codicia insaciable? Ilustres hazañas?" which appeared in the review *Escorial* in Spain, and was in turn attacked by Armando Bazán in the *Repertorio americano* of Costa Rica.

exclusively represents the complete Spanish genius. Even remembering the extraordinary and marvelous variety of men who made up the company of Spaniards in the New World, we come closer to the truth when we say: Spanish character was so fashioned that it can be likened to a medal stamped on each of its two sides with a strong and resolute face. One face is that of an imperialistic conquistador and the other is a friar devoted to God. Both these faces are undeniably and typically Spanish. Both friar and conquistador were imprisoned within the thinking of their own kind and their own time; neither when he was most himself could understand or forgive the other. Yet they were inseparably yoked, sent together into a new world and together were responsible for the action and achievement of Spain in America. To appreciate the full power and depth of Spanish character one must turn the medal and see both of these bold and purposeful Spanish faces. More, one must recognize as equally significant the attitude of the crown in permitting experiments and disputes of a most fundamental nature in those tumultuous years during which its policies and practices were evolving. It is to Spain's everlasting credit that she allowed men to insist that all her actions in America be just, and that at times she listened to these voices.

The struggle which Montesinos started is not yet over, in America or in the world. Thus the dust which covers the writing upon which these chapters are based cannot obscure the quality of life in the ideas and episodes set forth here. The cry of Montesinos denouncing the enslavement of the Indians, the loud voice of Bartolomé de Las Casas proclaiming that all the peoples of the world are men — these have not lost their validity today and they will still have it tomorrow. For in a sense they are timeless.

In the years since the ideals of justice for the American Indians were first enunciated and fought for, Spain has lost her empire, and the tread of Spanish soldiers no longer shakes the world, as it did in the sixteenth century. The horses of Cortés, which so amazed and frightened the hosts of Montezuma, have been superseded by steel tanks, and these in turn have been robbed of most of their significance by the atomic bomb. Just around the corner, we are told, are even greater atomic bombs and various instruments of bacterial warfare which will doubtless be as terrible a shock to our present age as was the first roar of the cannons of Cortés to the Aztecs armed only with arrows and spears.

Whatever means men develop, however, to destroy their fellow men, the real problems between nations do not lie in the realm of mechanics. They lie in the more difficult field of human relationships. Some Spaniards long ago discerned this truth, which the whole world must understand today if it is to survive. The specific methods used to apply the theories worked out by sixteenth-century Spaniards are now as outmoded as the blow guns with which Indians shot poisoned arrows at the conquistadores. But the ideals which some Spaniards sought to put into practice as they opened up the New World will never lose their shining brightness as long as men believe that other peoples have a right to live, that just methods may be found for the conduct of relations between peoples, and that essentially all the peoples of the world are men.

LIST OF WORKS CITED

AITON, ARTHUR S. "The secret visita against Viceroy Mendoza", *New Spain and the Anglo-American West*, I (Los Angeles, 1932) 1–22.

ANONYMOUS. "La locura de Fray Bartolomé de las Casas," *Revista hispanoamericana de ciencias, letras y artes*, VI (Madrid, 1927), 284–290.

BALLESTEROS GAIBROIS, MANUEL. "XXV Congreso internacional de americanistas," *Tierra firme*, I (Madrid, 1935), 133–38.

BARREDA Y LAOS, FELIPE. La vida intelectual de la colonia. Lima, 1909.

BLAKEY, ROBERT. History of Political Theory. 2 vols. London, 1855.

BOAS, FRANZ. „The history of anthropology," *Science*, XL (1904).

BOLÍVAR, SIMÓN. Discursos y proclamas. Paris, 1913. Ed. by Rufino Blanco-Fombona.

BOSWELL, JAMES. The Life of Samuel Johnson. 3 vols. London, 1924.

BOURNE, EDWARD G. "Columbus, Ramon Pane and the beginnings of American anthropology," *Proceedings of the American Antiquarian Society*, new series, XVII (1906), 310–48.

BROWN, JOHN L. The Methodus ad facilem historiarum cognitionem of Jean Bodin: a critical study. Washington, 1939.

CANNON, WALTER B. Bodily Changes in Pain, Hunger, Fear and Rage. New York, 1915.

CARBIA, RÓMULO D. La crónica oficial de las Indias Occidentales. Buenos Aires, 1940.

——. La superchería en la historia del descubrimiento de América, "*Humanidades*", XX (La Plata, 1930), 169–184.

——. Historia de la leyenda negra hispanoamericana. Buenos Aires, 1943.

CASAS, BARTOLOMÉ DE LAS. Apologética historia de las Indias. M. Serrano y Sanz, ed. Madrid, 1909.

——. Colección de tratados, 1552–1553. Buenos Aires, 1924. (Instituto de investigaciónes históricas).

——. Del único modo de atraer a todos los pueblos a la verdadera religión. México, 1942. Advertencia preliminar y edición y anotación por Agustín Millares Carlo. Versión española por Atenógenes Santamaría. Introducción por Lewis Hanke.

——. Historia de las Indias. 3 vols. Madrid, 1929(?). Ed. by Gonzalo de Reparaz.

CHACÓN Y CALVO, JOSÉ MARÍA. Cartas censorias de la conquista. La Habana, 1938.

——. Cedulario cubano. Los orígenes de la colonización (1493–1512). Madrid, 1930(?).

——. Criticismo y colonización. La Habana, 1935.

——. La experiencia del indio. Un antecedente a las doctrinas de Vitoria? Madrid, 1934.

Díaz del Castillo, Bernal. Historia verdadera de la conquista de la Nueva España. 2 vols. México, 1943. Ed. by Ramón Iglesia.

Documentos inéditos de América. Colección de documentos inéditos, relativos al descubrimiento, conquista, y organización de las antiguas posesiones españolas en América y Oceania. 42 tomos. Madrid, 1864–1884.

DuBois, William E. B. Black Reconstruction. New York, 1935.

Ercilla y Zûñiga, Alonso de. La Araucana. Salamanca, 1574.

Ernst, James. Roger Williams. New York, 1932.

Esquivel Obregón, Toribio. Apuntes para la historia de derecho en México. 3 vols. México, 1937–43.

Estudios de historiografía de la Nueva España. Con una introducción de Ramón Iglesia. México, 1945.

Fabié, Antonio María. Vida y escritos de don Fray Bartolomé de las Casas. 2 vols. Madrid, 1879.

Fernández, León. Colección de documentos para la historia de Costa Rica. 10 vols. San José, 1881–1917.

Fernández de Navarrete, Martín. Colección de los viajes y descubrimientos que hicieron por mar los españoles desde fines del siglo XV. 5 vols. Madrid, 1825–37.

Fletcher, Robert. „Paul Broca and the French school of anthropology," *The Saturday lectures delivered in the lecture room of the U.S. National Museum under the auspices of the anthropological and biological societies of Washington* (Washington, 1882), 113-142.

Fuentes y Guzmán, Francisco Antonio de. Recordación florida .... 3 vols. Guatemala, 1933.

Giménez Fernández, Manuel. Nuevas consideraciones sobre la historia, sentido y valor de las bulas alejandrinas de 1493 referentes a las Indias. Sevilla, 1944.

Gay Calbó, Enrique. „Discurso sobre Fray Bartolomé de las Casas," *Boletín del archivo nacional*, XLI (La Habana, 1942), 100–106.

Hanke, Lewis. La lucha por la justicia en la conquista de América. Buenos Aires, 1949. Editorial Sudamericana.

——. The Spanish Struggle for Justice in the Conquest of America. Philadelphia, 1949. University of Pennsylvania Press.

——. Las teorías políticas de Bartolomé de las Casas. Buenos Aires, 1935. (Instituto de investigaciones históricas).

——. "Francisco Toledo and the just titles of Spain to the Inca empire," *The Americas*, III (Washington, 1946), 3–19.

——. "Dos palabras on Antonio de Ulloa and the Noticias Secretas," *Hispanic American Historical Review*, XVI (1936), 479–514.

——. (Ed.) Cuerpo de documentos del siglo XVI sobre los derechos de España en las Indias y las Filipinas. México, 1943. (En colaboración con Agustín Millares Carlo).

——. "Free speech in sixteenth-century America", *Hispanic American Historical Review*, XXVI (1946), 135–49.

—. The First Social Experiments in America. Cambridge, Massachusetts, 1935.

HELPS, ARTHUR. The Spanish Conquest in America and its relation to the history of slavery and the government of colonies. 4 vols. London, 1855–61.

HENRÍQUEZ-UREÑA, PEDRO. Literary Currents in Hispanic America. Cambridge, Massachusetts, 1945.

HUMBOLDT, ALEXANDER VON. Political Essay on the Kingdom of New Spain. 4 vols. London, 1811–1822.

IGLESIA, RAMÓN. Cronistas e historiadores de la conquista de México. México, 1942.

LARRAZABAL BLANCO, CARLOS. "Bibliografía colonial. Fray Bartolomé de Las Casas," *Clio*, IX (Ciudad Trujillo, 1941).

LEVENE, RICARDO. Introducción a la historia del derecho indiano. Buenos Aires, 1924.

LEVILLIER, ROBERTO, Don Francisco de Toledo, supremo organizador del Perú; su vida, su obra (1515–1582). 3 vols. Buenos Aires, 1935–42.

LEVY-BRUHL, LUCIEN. How natives think. New York, 1926.

LOTHROP, SAMUEL K. Coclé, an archaeological study. Cambridge, Massachusetts, 1937.

MARTÍ, JOSÉ. Obras completas. Edición commemorativa del cincuentenario de su muerte. Prólogo y síntesis biográfica por M. Isidro Méndez. 2 vols. La Habana, 1946.

MARETT, ROBERT R. Tylor. New York, 1936.

MATTHEWS, WASHINGTON. "The study of ethics among the lower races," *Journal of American folklore*, XII (1899).

MEDINA, JOSÉ TORIBIO. El descubrimiento del Océano Pacífico. 3 vols. Santiago, 1913–20.

MENDIETA, JERÓNIMO DE. Historia eclesiástica indiana. México, 1870. Ed. by Joaquín García Icazbalceta.

MENÉNDEZ PIDAL, RAMÓN. "Codicia insaciable? Ilustres hazañas?", *Escorial*, I (Madrid, 1940), no. 1.

MITCHELL, WESLEY (ed.). What Veblen Taught. New York, 1936.

MORISON, SAMUEL ELIOT. Admiral of the Ocean Sea. 2 vols. Boston, 1942.

MOTOLINÍA, FR. TORIBIO DE BENAVENTE O. Historia de los indios de la Nueva España. Barcelona, 1914. Ed. by Daniel Sánchez García.

MUÑOZ Y MANZANO, CIPRIANO (Conde de Viñaza). Bibliografía española de lenguas indígenas de América. Madrid, 1892.

MYRES, JOHN L. "The influence of anthropology on the course of political science," *Report of the British Association for the Advancement of Science*, 1909 (London, 1910).

NORTHROP, F. S. C. The Meeting of East and West. New York, 1946.

O'GORMAN, EDMUNDO. Fundamentos de la historia de América. México, 1942.

——. "Sobre la naturaleza bestial del indio americano", *Filosofía y letras*, No. 1 (México, 1941), 141–158; No. 2: 303–315.

ORTIZ Y FERNÁNDEZ, FERNANDO. El engaño de las razas. La Habana, 1945.

OVIEDO Y VALDÉS, GONZALO FERNÁNDEZ DE. Historia general y natural de las Indias, islas y Tierra Firme del Mar Océano. 4 vols. Madrid, 1851–55. Ed. by José Amador de los Ríos.

PARKER, THEODORE. Collected works. 12 vols. London, 1863–65.

RECINOS, ADRIÁN. Popul Vuh. México, 1947.

REMESAL, ANTONIO DE. Historia general de las Indias Occidentales, y particular de la gobernación de Chiapas y Guatemala. Madrid, 1619.

RICARD, ROBERT. La 'Conquête spirituelle' du Mexique. Paris, 1933.

RÍOS, FERNANDO DE LOS. "The religious character of colonial law in sixteenth-century Spain," *Proceedings of the sixth international congress of philosophy,* 1926 (1927).

RIVERA Y SANROMÁN, AGUSTÍN. Principios críticos sobre el virreinato de la Nueva España i sobre la revolución de independencia. 3 cols. Lagos, 1884–1888.

ROBERTSON, WILLIAM. History of America. 2 vols. London, 1777.

SACO, JOSÉ ANTONIO. "La Historia de las Indias por Fray Bartolomé de las Casas, y la Real Academia de la Historia de Madrid," *Revista hispano-americana de Madrid* (Feb. 12, 1865). Reprinted by Saco in his *Historia de la esclavitud de la raza africana en el mundo nuevo y en especial en los paises américo-hispanos,* I (Barcelona, 1879), Apéndice 5, pp. 373–380.

SAHAGÚN, BERNARDINO DE. Historia general de las cosas de Nueva España. 5 vols. México, 1938. Ed. by Wigberto Jiménez Moreno.

SCHLAIFER, ROBERT O. "Greek theories of slavery from Homer to Aristotle," *Harvard Studies in Classical Philology,* No. 27 (Cambridge, Massachusetts, 1936), 165–204.

SERRANO Y SANZ, MANUEL. "Doctrinas psicológicas de Fr. Bartolomé de las Casas," *Revista de archivos, bibliotecas, y museos,* XVII (Madrid, 1907), 59–79.

SHATTUCK, GEORGE C. "Syphilis in Yucatan," *The Peninsula of Yucatan* (Washington, 1932), 249–289.

SIKES, E. E. Anthropology of the Greeks. London, 1914.

SIMPSON, LESLEY B. The Encomienda in New Spain. Berkeley, 1929.

SOLÓRZANO Y PEREIRA, JUAN DE. Política indiana. Madrid, 1648.

SOUTHEY, ROBERT. History of Brazil. London, 1817.

STEVENS, HENRY (ed.). The New Laws of the Indies. London, 1893.

STREIT, ROBERT. "Fr. Ramon Pane, der erste Etnograph Amerikas", *Zeitschrift fur Missionswissenschaft,* X (Münster i w., 1920.

TICKNOR, GEORGE. History of Spanish Literature. 3 vols. Boston, 1872.

TOZZER, ALFRED M. (ed.) Landa's Relación de las cosas de Yucatán. Cambridge, Massachusetts, 1941.

WHITE, LESLIE A. "Evolucionismo e anti-evolucionismo na teoria etnológica americana," *Sociologia,* X (São Paulo, 1948), 1–39.

WILSON, WOODROW. The Public Papers of Woodrow Wilson. 6 vols. New York, 1925–27. Edited by Ray Stannard Baker and William E. Dodd.

WOLCOTT, ROGER, (ed.) Correspondence of William Hickling Prescott. Boston, 1925.

ZAVALA, SILVIO "¿Las Casas, esclavista?", *Cuadernos americanos,* año 3 (México, 1944), No. 2: 149–154.

——. Filosofía de la conquista. México, 1947.

——. New Viewpoints on the Spanish Colonization of America. Philadelphia, 1943.

INDEX

OTHER WORKS BY THE AUTHOR ON BARTOLOMÉ DE LAS CASAS

1935

Las teorías políticas de Bartolomé de Las Casas. Buenos Aires, 65 p. (Publicaciones de la Sección de Historia de la Facultad de Filosofía y Letras de la Universidad de Buenos Aires).

1941

,,Un festón de documentos lascasasianos'', *Revista cubana* (La Habana), t. 15: 150–211.

1942

Bartolomé de Las Casas. Del único modo de atraer a todos los pueblos a la verdadera religión. México. Fondo de Cultura Económica. XLIV, 594 p. Advertencia preliminar y edición y anotación del texto por Agustín Millares Carlo. Introducción por Lewis Hanke. Versión española por Atenógenes Santamaría.

,,Las Casas y Sepúlveda en la controversia de Valladolid'', *Universidad Católica bolivariana* (Medellín, Colombia), t. 8: 65–96.

1943

Cuerpo de documentos del siglo XVI sobre los derechos de España en las Indias y las Filipinas, descubiertos y anotados por Lewis Hanke. México: Fondo de Cultura Económica. 364 p. Ed. por Agustín Millares Carlo.

1949

The Spanish Struggle for Justice in the Conquest of America. Philadelphia: University of Pennsylvania Press. 217 p.

La lucha por la justicia en la conquista española de América. Buenos Aires. Editorial Sudamericana. 572 p.

,,Interpretaciones de la obra y significación de Bartolomé de Las Casas, desde el siglo XVI hasta nuestros días'', *Latinoamérica,* año 1, no. 7 (Julio, México).

84679

H